AF305212

Mind of the Raven:
Investigations and Adventures with Wolf-Birds

Racing the Antelope:
What Animals Can Teach Us About Running and Life
(later republished as Why We Run: A Natural History*)*

Winter World:
The Ingenuity of Animal Survival

The Geese of Beaver Bog

The Snoring Bird:
My Family's Journey Through a Century of Biology

Summer World:
A Season of Bounty

The Nesting Season:
Cuckoos, Cuckolds, and the Invention of Monogamy

The Common Uncommon

A Forest Journey

Bernd Heinrich

W. W. NORTON & COMPANY

Independent Publishers Since 1923

*For my father, Gerd H. Heinrich,
and all parents who survived adversity
and made the best of opportunities*

CONTENTS

Part IV   Remembering

Part V   Returning

PREFACE

RADITIONALLY, A STORY STARTS FROM A PROBLEM or a place and continues to an ending or a conclusion. This one is not traditional. It starts at a place but reaches out from there forward, back, and in between. It did not begin with a destination other than the pure adventure of it. Absence of a goal is freedom to notice the new that comes along, rather than continuing on a path to what one had preconceived.

I have been ensconced here for forty years in the Maine woods, in my log cabin. I've explored all around, been affected by changes, concentrated on specific differences, and picked up on what came along that I've seen. These tended to be the "common uncommon" because they had not been sufficiently noticed. Birds count in this, as do spiders, chestnut trees, porcupines, and myriad other observations. Even after sixty years, I am still shown surprises, but no single one steals the show. They arrive and leave me open to others that are new, unexpected, and sometimes delighting.

The Common Uncommon

Cycles

Although research proceeds from one step to another, the sequence taken is often not as logical nor as linear as the book that results. I had, in the beginning, no grand model or design in mind, to be corroborated by a planned set of experiments in the field and in the laboratory. I pursued only small questions that seemed interesting in light of previously collected data. The central theme presented here . . . emerged of its own accord.

BUMBLEBEE ECONOMICS, 1979

A EUGLENA (GENUS *EUGLENA*) IS A SINGLE-CELLED organism that is part animal, part plant. It swims in fresh waters by whipping a flagellum at its hind end like a tail and uses its mitochondria to process sugar as an energy source to move, grow, and divide to reproduce. Yet, in the presence of light, like plants, it grows chloroplasts to capture energy and turn green.

Every euglena in the world is a copy of one that over a hundred million years ago became a green cell and benefited over another that didn't. Every day and night, with cycles of light and dark, the euglena doubles and becomes two—just as every summer, the trees and bees are generating themselves into what will become them again almost exactly. Each will insert itself into something beyond, of greater dimension and larger scope. The same is true for animals, including we humans. None of us can live alone. We are *all* intimately connected with other life. If you love the forest, it is something you can become a physical (rather than just an inevitable global atomic) part of. I hope, someday, to become a part of the whole of the Everlasting, and specifically the woods I love most.

MEANWHILE, THE CYCLES I've come to know are shifting as the sad truth of climate change, with its decimating effects, progresses. The solution to what appears a looming crisis will not come from this president or that corporation; our enemy is not a nation or ideology, one against the other. This time we are all aboard the same lifeboat—a tiny one, like a cell, given the cosmos with respect to planet Earth. We are all the consumers contributing to what has been ongoing and moving at an ever-faster rate. Only relative "seconds" ago in the overall seasons of our existence, we saw almost all the forest as an evil wild thing to cut down to make way for human home and industry. We've seen the prairies melt away, feeding cities where there had been forests, the lungs of the earth. The physiology of the planet, a superorganism of which we are but a small part physically—each a euglena in a woodland pond—is being disrupted in its working parts.

There are ever-diminishing exceptions. Compared with other states, Maine is little changed since John Cabot first visited in 1497 or since I first moved here over seventy-three years ago. Its forests can serve as a model of what once was, what to keep, and what to strive to restore. Admittedly, our northern habitat, the state of Maine especially, has a natural advantage: It is still a model of nature as it ought to be. Of its twenty-three million acres, seventeen and a half million are forest cover, with

82 percent of that area still containing a rich fauna of its original populations of moose, deer, black bear, lynx, bobcats, otter, beaver, bald eagles, ravens, goshawks, grouse, and most of the other small birds, plus now more Canada geese, since we've reduced hunting pressure on them and allowed them to nest in our cities, where there are fewer predators. Maine's caribou population left only recently—in the early 1900s—due to the return of the forest after the last glaciation over twenty thousand years ago, and instead we now have a healthy population of turkeys. Moose declined in the late 1800s, and bear had been almost eradicated by 1900; credit for their reappearance in the forest after deforestation through farming and logging goes to the regrowth of their preferred habitat of broad-leaved trees, as well as to wildlife conservation laws.

Just as much, what is keeping Maine green perhaps is the not-so-easy-to-live-in ecosystem, which includes the insect guard, starting with the bloodsucking blackflies, which in June can be near horrendous, as acknowledged on a T-shirt that I own. It shows a blackfly caricature with an ugly face, labeled "Defender of the Wilderness." It further notes, "A bite of the proceeds will be bled into the Maine Blackfly Breeders Association, a not-for-profit association."

However, I feel even more averse to the tick abundance in early spring for the various diseases they carry. One species kills a significant percentage of the moose population each winter by sheer bloodletting, leaving red trails on the snow. More apparent to me are the tiny buzzers that pester in late summer after the deerflies, what I call "eye-flies" for their uncanny brazen persistence to put themselves, as mere specks, into your eyes. All are guardians of the wilderness, as are the preponderance of rocks of all shapes and sizes left by the glaciers that in some areas make moving at anything other than the speed of a forest a chore.

ONE SUMMER IN the early 1960s, during my undergraduate studies as a forestry major at the University of Maine in Orono, I had the memorable experience of working an entire season in a lumber camp in the seemingly endless forest of the Allagash wilderness region of northern Maine. The camp consisted of the traditional log-walled cabins used to house the crews, horses, an eating place for the communal meals, cooking hall, office, and outhouses. Every logger had a horse for twitching out the individual trees designated with a paint mark to be cut with chain saws and axes. All this was replaced a few years later by the monster machine that put people out of work, created clear-cuts, and eradicated the ancient conifers; the poplars then shot up, followed by the tick explosion that kills the moose in winter.

The way trees are harvested now is profoundly different (and with a far greater impact) from the way my parents and Susie lumbered seventy years ago. Susie was a fine horse, as workhorses go, for pulling out a log when there were no snowdrifts to interfere. However, since colonial times the standard for hauling out trees was a team of two oxen. Forty-five years ago, I'd still hired a driver and his team to move the red spruces I had felled for the walls of my cabin, moving them into a clearing that had once been a cow pasture.

Such logging, which was once a serious and essential Northern Forest protocol, has become mere symbolic work. It became as emblematic of logging as throwing the javelin, which was once a skill of war made superfluous by torpedo squadrons, nuclear bombs, and guided missiles. And so it is in the war on the forest: The horse, then oxen, the crosscut saw and axe, even the chain saw faded out as the monstrous feller-buncher operated by levers in a sealed cab grasps, cuts, and lifts the limbs and then stacks the lumber into neat rows. I checked the Internet about buying a used one and found a listing of twenty-one for sale. The 2018 model was priced at $499,000 and one three years older could be had for less than half that: $210,850. A good new chain saw can be bought for a thousand times less. What this means is that small landowners, such as those with perhaps several hundred acres, will become exempt from being logged because the investment will not cover the costs—except on an industrial scale. What was then was unique. It was something for everyman or everywoman. Shame on progress, which appears to be ever distancing from the forest, the fount of life on land.

As the relationship with the land has been severed by the so-called progress of replacing people with machines, there is ever less chance of getting close to nature, becoming acquainted with the chickadees, blue jays, and maybe an occasional grouse. That bond, or severing of it, will have an effect on the future of the forest, and in that sense, given all the sales of used feller-bunchers, that future has already happened. Popular publications like *Northern Woodlands* push back, catering to ever-more people who have been able to escape the cities to pursue their dream of owning a small woods plot, but less for making their living there than finding enjoyment in and of it.

I think of Robert Frost's poem "Mowing," of love of the land where his scythe is "whispering" through the grass and it being "the sweetest dream that labor knows" to make hay while seeing "feeble-pointed spikes of flowers . . . and scared a bright green snake." What can we see mowing forest trees while captive in a bubble? What is the future of that in the Northern Forest? What would it bring in, and what take out? The "energy crisis" is a population crisis of too many people, rather than a lack of deployment of more technology to provide more energy. The short-term solutions that we are so vigorously pursuing create problems up ahead. Thinking in terms of decades is shortsighted unless it includes the whole. The solution will not come from this president or that corporation, but rather from empathy.

GETTING TO KNOW animals of other species leads to empathy with them and perhaps sometimes to putting them into their place in an iconic identity. There are Indigenous "People of the Deer" and of Bear, Eagle, and Raven because of intimate associations that revealed the otherwise not seen similarities.

One of my most vivid memories as a budding biologist taking my first steps toward pursuing a professional career was the stressful interviewing for admission to a PhD graduate degree at the University of New York at Buffalo. The interviewing professor started out with the most natural and obvious question: "Why do you want be a biologist?" I responded with the first thing that came to mind, which was my experience with bumblebees. As a child, I'd crossed the babbling brook by our cabin in the Hahnheide nature reserve in Germany on my way to the village school when I stopped in my tracks under a huge willow tree. In full flower, it was loaded with yellow catkins and buzzing from the activity of many bumblebees. I was mesmerized and had to see them closer. I studied their brown fuzz and the yellow pollen loads they carried on their hind legs. Warblers fresh back from migration were calling sweetly in the same tree, and I remember it all even now, seven decades later. My interviewer rose from his chair and declared: "You are a *naturalist*" and that was the end of the interview. I later learned that this meant to him that I was not a scientist. Scientists worked in the *lab* with test tubes and studied DNA, not fuzzy brown bees and birdsong.

As it turned out, however, I would by chance and then by one circumstance after another study DNA, because I had no money and worked in a lab washing glassware for my eventual hero, professor James R. Cook. Because of him I received a full stipend to UCLA, where I tried for one year as a PhD candidate to extract DNA from *Euglena gracilis*. These protozoa would end up having large implications on my worldview, but at the time just resulted in my "flunking out" after a year because I didn't succeed with the DNA. This set me on a new path that led to unfathomed discoveries, resulting in some hundred or so scientific publications in leading journals and with a benefit of seeing the world in research and residencies in Germany, Israel, Suriname, Costa Rica, Alaska, New Guinea, Ellesmere Island, four countries in Africa, California deserts, Vermont, and, of course, the Maine woods.

I credit my discoveries to intimate contact with nature, perhaps by first watching bumblebees in the field and then going from there. Curiosity, love, and inspiration lead to looking closely and finding wonders that may lead to morphology, physiology, behavior, ecology, or evolution, if not the meaning of Life. Bumblebees in the Northern Forest of Maine were responsible for this book, initially observed from as close as ten yards from where I now sit as I write this, and where I am a part of this forest and anticipate becoming so literally.

Every euglena in the world is a copy of one that over hundreds of millions of years ago entered a cell of some sort that then benefited more than another that didn't. Every day it not only lives on but may double and become two. Every summer the trees and the bees generate something of themselves that will become them closely but not exactly. Each will insert itself and become something beyond itself—a part of *that* something and for life. If you love the forest, it becomes a part of you.

Part I

Being

One

Entering the Forest

*I ramble in my home woods at different times and circumstances.
I've struck out in the middle of a blizzard. Once in July I waited
until midnight to head out. I've wandered out on spring dawns just
when the warblers were returning, on sweltering summer afternoons
when the blackflies were biting, in thunderstorms and also under
blue sunny skies in Indian summer when the woods were a kaleidoscope of brilliant colors. In my memory, I savor the images that
were collected on these rambles and that bind me to this place. Some
might consider these images trifles. But I am hard-pressed to come
up with greater riches. . . .*

THE TREES IN MY FOREST, *1997*

ONE MIGHT THINK I WOULD RUN OUT OF THINGS
to see, learn, and explore when I step out of my cabin.
Instead, every observation is in the context of the similar or the
different at some past time or in relation to something else. The
expected provides a standard, and the more acutely drawn from
experience, the more the differences stand out. This is true for at
least one thing every day, and there is hardly a day in my week
derived from a preplanned schedule, which creates the freedom
to notice something new. But that *new* is, at times, predicated on
what came before. I am fond of the English philosopher and biologist Herbert Spencer's quote of 1860 in *Education: Intellectual,*

Moral, and Physical: "Whoever has not in youth collected plants and insects, knows not half the halo of interest which lanes and hedgerows can assume. . . . where imbedded treasures were found." I have been led to those "lanes and hedgerows" and found more than one can imagine, and I hope to share some of that journey in and of the forever changing biology and spectacle of the Northern Forest that is boundless.

In winter I can't wait until spring, then in summer I look forward to the fresh breezes of autumn when the leaves light up in a blaze of yellows, reds, purple. Fruits are ripening and the birds are overhead migrating day and night, guided by the sun and stars on their mind-boggling journeys. Then a day arrives when some snow crystals drift tranquilly down, as if nature is going to sleep, but at some point, raging storms follow that challenge the trees right down to the roots, and I know it will be a long haul until spring.

In my writing, I aim to provide a feel for the Northern Forest in the context of its hugely seasonal background, but with prognosis into the future. I focus on the life of this forest from connections in everyday living in all seasons in and around my home in these mountains of western Maine. I examine the life encountered during recent real walks in this virtual walk through the forest by my cabin since retiring here. I hope to provide a fresh look into the western mountains of Maine through foresight and hindsight.

Covering an expanse of about 6.6 million square miles, the Northern, or Boreal, Forest is a vast sea of spruce, fir, and larch, with birch and poplar mixed in, that stretches north to the treeless tundra and the grass steppes of Siberia and North America. Southward it blends into a mix with deciduous broad-leaved trees that annually shed their leaves. Similar plant progressions occur by altitude on the mountains, along with the forest's famed denizens, the wolf, coyote, moose, black bear, lynx, snowshoe hare, tick, mosquito, midge, deerfly, and blackfly. It is a land of winter snow and ice storms, summer heat and, at times, fire, drought, and floods. All life in this immense forest confronts vast and sometimes rapid changes as one season (and even one day) brings with it a different environment, so much so that its plants and animals have evolved to cope not only with the seasonal extremes, but with the often large changes occurring *within* them.

Weather makes the seasons, but it is also often contrary to them. Where I have lived in my cabin in the Maine woods for the past sixty-five years, I have experienced tree-killing snowstorms in early June after the trees have leafed out. There are Christmases without snow, and there is rain turning to ice in January. Along with preparations for the seasons, plants and animals respond to the weather, or are responded to, facing life-threatening situations that to us can seem only bothersome as we sit before our fireplaces, cast-iron stoves, propane burners, and furnaces fueled by wood, coal, or oil. Having felt the cold, and at times the heat as well, while living in the woods full-time, I am naturally curious, and sometimes astounded, by what behaviors and physiology can accomplish to make this habitat not just our home, but much more so.

Most of my life's focus is on this forest tract of about five hundred acres where I grew up and then settled. It is secured under a Maine Forest Society easement, which designates what is and is not allowed. A century ago, here was a huge farmstead of orchards and stone wall–enclosed pastures for cattle, then sheep. My land has remnants of five old seasonal camps, aside from its farm homesites, although there is barely a trace of a residence ever having been there, except when a close search reveals the remains of a wheel and axle of an automobile, or a trace of a chimney gradually returning into the soil and becoming clothed in dense forest, or stone walls that were once cattle and sheep fences. The one-acre clearing I live in is reserved for agriculture and two minimalist dwellings along with the typical farm garden that takes some doing every year to keep down the weeds and the competing young maple, birch, ash, poplar, and cherry trees. It is an expanse of two species of goldenrod, fireweed, milkweed, blackberry, raspberry, and blueberry, as well as six species of other berry bushes, primarily viburnums.

The human presence has increased ecological diversity. Mine is an "artificial" oasis and the only place in the acreage where monarch butterflies, bumblebees, yellow-throated and chestnut-sided warblers, indigo buntings, tree swallows, a pair of bluebirds, and green snakes reside. It also contains a dug hole, now a pool where several species of frog and spotted salamander spawn, the larval home where damselflies, dragonflies, water skimmers, giant water beetles, water bugs, mayflies, and mosquitoes are generated. This open space is the only place for miles where the wood-cocks sky dance in spring, as they need a treeless landing space in between successive courtship flights.

As far as I know, nobody was ever critical of the facilities at my log cabin at the west end of the old farm. There is no such thing as a hot shower, but there is running water. It comes from a rock-lined fifteen-foot-deep well dug a century or two earlier, now only a hundred yards into the encroaching woods. Some years it has gone dry, and when it did, I descended to the bottom, stepping on the stones of its wall as a ladder. There were no skeletons at the bottom, just various farm implements (an axe, a bark spud used for peeling bark off fresh tree trunks, a chain, and various minor trinkets). The well had been *well* used for the kitchen and the cattle. It is the only water source within a half mile, until it rains or snows in the winter.

The current outhouse is usually a mere minutes' walk from the front door, although distance varies, depending on where the next hole is dug. The seat is deliberately situated for maximum forest and sunrise view, and over the years the neighboring field had been an apple orchard pruned out to favor maturing maple trees that are used for tapping. I wondered at one time if I would live to see them to this stage and am now delighted that I can get ten times more syrup than needed strictly dependent on effort.

The camp parties with University of Vermont students are not so loud and rowdy as when a hundred or so eager helpers volunteered to build a giant aviary into the nearby woods and then later showed up again for the raven roundups to populate it and produce the wing-tagged and radio-labeled birds. The hundreds we trapped revealed much more than we thought possible, and I won't forget them—helpers and birds—as emissaries of the wild. Nor will I forget Jamie Wyeth trudging up the hill with a huge packet of shrimp to one of our parties, asking to see ravens or photos of them to paint, and I suggested better: dropping a dead cow in front of his window by his lighthouse. He got what he wanted, and I did too—an original painting of one of those ravens that visited *his* cow.

The huge wooden table in the log cabin has become crowded with signatures carved into it by most of the visitors. A note when I'm not at home states: "Have a beer, that is here and carve your name on the table." Solar panels now provide power for electric lights—a vast improvement since I started with a kerosene lamp, which went extinct with the invention of the propane lamp, then the electric from a car battery, to now solar panels. No one step to the other had ever been imagined. I'm now mostly hampered by all of the electrical marvels, as it turns out they are inadequate for everything that used to be simple, doable, not costing a fortune, and which never once caused headaches without a solution.

I HAVE STAYED a near lifetime associated with a specific area of wild forest in these mountains. Papa lost everything, including his mother, in World War II. He fought in both world wars after enlisting to save his life, and often declared that cities are bomb targets, but the woods aren't—they are full of treasures. The biggest treasures for me in Hahnheide—the forest we escaped to—were bird nests. One I recall specifically was that of a wood thrush up in a spruce tree I climbed. To my surprise, the sky-blue eggs were nestled on metal tinsel like we'd found in the woods and used to decorate our Christmas tree. I later learned that the tinsel had come from the sky. It had been dropped to disrupt radar of the bomber attacks that burned and leveled nearby Hamburg. Planting trees has always given me a positive feeling, an act for the future, and indeed, when I now see an alley of trees I've planted from seedlings, it makes me feel good.

My memories of Maine date back to age twelve in 1952. One of my first memories is of a porcupine in an oak tree that's within jogging distance of my cabin now. That tree is still in place, but there were then no wild turkeys in New England. Porcupines remain as before, and I got to know a baby one almost immediately, and loved to pet it, of course only stroking it in one direction. It reminded me of the European always comical "hedgehog," or as we called it, *Igel*, that could roll into a ball for protection, whereas the porcupine instead slaps you with its thickly muscled tail armed with spines, whose ends are like tenacious fishhooks.

Within months of my family's arrival from Germany, my new native Mainer friends, Floyd Adams and Phil Potter, introduced me to fishing for perch, catfish, bass, and sunfish in our nearby Pease Pond, and then to the sport of finding bee nests in hollow trees in the fall, when the goldenrod was in bloom just before the wild asters' flower buds opened in blue splendor. Grouse and deer hunting would start soon, along with the kaleidoscope of colored leaves falling. In summer I had picked tomato hornworms off our neighbors' plants, and Phil Potter taught me how to trap the long-tailed white weasel to sell its fur, as he had done as a teenager. It was all like an impossible dream come true.

It is no mystery that I bonded so quickly to the forest where our family had landed by events that astound me still. But then, after just one idyllic year in the Maine paradise with our neighbors and our soon-owned equally idyllic farm, my parents left for six years hunting birds for the Yale Peabody Museum. They were capitalizing on their previous experience hunting birds in the jungles of Indonesia, Persia (Iran), and Burma (Myanmar), which they did for various museums, including the American Museum of Natural History in New York, which we as a family visited on the day we stepped off the *Batory*, an ocean liner that passed the Statue of Liberty before docking in New York City. The AMNH already contained many specimens from my father's long-standing contributions to the study of ichneumon wasps and other creatures of decades previous, whetting my passion for contact with nature in the wild—an experience that could only be imagined then but would eventually happen.

What actually followed for me and my younger sister Marianne was six years at a boarding school for disadvantaged kids. While potentially an ideal environment—some three thousand acres of prime Northern Forest along the Kennebec River—yet I sorely missed my former freedom of the wild and chafed from domesticity with a dorm mother demanding house chores daily. In spirit I was more in line with Tarzan of the Apes. So I ran away to go back home (near where I live now) in the woods by Mount Tumbledown. I was sixteen, and Mamuscha—my mother—(in a letter I found recently) declared that my letters (to her in Africa) were "those of a ten-year-old, in penmanship and in text." Admittedly, I cared for neither. But due to luck and circumstance, I nevertheless ended up with a University of Maine master's degree (with a thesis on *Euglena*) that the faculty awarded me "with distinction" and even had me give a departmental lecture on my work. This paved the way for a fellowship and a PhD at UCLA (with a thesis on the tomato hornworm moth) that was also awarded the same accolade, but this one had followed a full year of total failure on a project that had *not* been based on observations from the wild. My unexpected success with the tomato hornworms had been possible from my direct contact with nature. In this case it was ultimately derived from weeding the gardens of my youth and having been familiar with the hornworm caterpillars that I'd then raised as a teenager to see become huge moths for my collection.

My mother had not been happy with me running away from boarding school after having been there only four years, and she never forgave me. She was also not happy years later when I returned home during the summer break from teaching at UC Berkeley with my then wife Kitty, our shepherd dog Foonman, and two pet ravens. When we arrived at the farm, my mother made sure I wouldn't inherit it, as I had foolishly thought I might. So I asked Mike Graham, a real estate agent (and previous dormmate at the University of Maine), to keep an eye out for me for a lot to build a cabin on, no matter how small it might be. It ended up much larger than expected and up in the hills precisely where Floyd and Phil—my everlasting friends and mentors—had introduced me to the Maine woods.

THE LAND I settled on was called Adams Hill, although it then changed names and became York. I don't care what its name is, as long as all my friends know *it* is, and it is Nature's. I'm not sure how one should own land, or air or water, except to love and respect it for what it is. I had loved it decades before I'd lived it, but I knew what it was long before even then.

It was, until the 1930s, a dairy farm with two huge barns and an impressively large manor next to an orchard of the Ben Davis apples, known as "a good keeper," a variety that resisted spoilage and was shipped (literally) to England. When I first went there (a year before boarding school), several mature trees remained, although the brush from the seeds of the surrounding forest had grown for several decades, and the site was ideal habitat for anything that liked to eat apples: deer, bear, grouse, porcupines. The adjacent landscape of overgrown pastures was a mix of coniferous and deciduous trees, with enough space between to allow blueberries to spread. I was undecided for a while on whether to clear the brush and trees to make a blueberry field or to let the trees grow. I let the trees grow and have since sold a harvest of pine logs.

Another pasture on the west side of the hill was much farther along in the natural progression, and the pines there are now likely among the largest in the state. They have been placed under official protection "into perpetuity" by the Forest Society of Maine, which owns the easement. Other sections of the forest are officially designated "growing wild," either totally (no forest intervention permitted) or "logging permitted" under the supervision of a forester, whose mission is to maintain a forest, such as I am doing personally when I'm harvesting firewood. With modest amounts needed (six or seven cords per year), I can be choosy and get enough wood close to the path that I can carry it to my truck. I favor dead or dying trees, especially those that are small, such as spruce and balsam fir, considered the most abundant in the state of Maine. They grow quickly and die quickly too, even if they are in full sunlight and without competition.

With no pressure of industrial harvesting, requiring massive amounts of logs taken in a short time from a large space, I can be selective. I have a reason for every tree taken, and the question I always ask myself before cutting is, "How will it affect the future growth at that place?" Because in this forest there is potential for any of a dozen tree species, and a hundred individuals can sprout from almost any square yard. But I normally choose between one or another tree of the mix that has already been selected by the forest itself over the last decades. I can help it along on its innate trajectory and at the same time express biases—for example, to keep it forest as opposed to something like a corn crop—the choices embracing a future and acknowledging a past. That means that my over-five-hundred-year-old yellow birch that is hollow will stay. And a big white birch that is two arms' length around the trunk is a unique individual not to be sacrificed when there are so many others that will help younger trees grow. Near this thick birch is another that is thin and that reaches even higher, but it has been leaning toward one side, toward an opening in the forest canopy and shading a young chestnut tree nearby. The tall thin birch has little future compared with others, some even standing tall. So, as I look around, I decide that *this* may be the one to take, helping that well-placed American native chestnut reach the sunshine in the spring.

Each forest develops into a unity, from small to ever-larger relationships and the niches it provides for sun from above the ground in the canopy, to the water it holds in and on the ground, in its vernal pool puddles and its competition. Further, I consider the landscape, the woodcocks' dancing field, the field for flowers for bees. Also, I consider water. And for me at camp, the closest puddle is one that I'd dug to attract a pair of wood ducks and perhaps water striders, dragonflies, mayflies, but not too many mosquitoes. Wood frogs were not on my mind and became a first great gift of nature at a time when I had the experience and knowledge to have something to look for in them and hopefully to see. They came to the pool first thing in the spring, and they cannot be missed because their presence is announced by a loud communal chorus and an orgy of mating and egg laying for several days.

The pool holds a literal cloud of thousands of tadpoles and froglets before fall, which the broad-winged hawks nesting nearby feed their young on. Fair enough, as in the fall I'd be feeding on the trees for wood, sugar syrup, and the black cherries so many birds like, too, as well as a deer (hopefully) that would have fed on the young chestnut trees growing in the forest, amid the thousands of frogs feeding on every insect in sight, which feed on me.

Two

Like Drops of Sap into a Bucket

We bond to what we become close to, in this case the young sap-sucker, but we also bond to our surroundings—the nature this bird represented.

A Naturalist at Large, 2018

I DOUBTED I'D LIVE LONG ENOUGH TO BE ABLE TO HARvest maple syrup here, but one day I decided to give it a try. There was brush of just about every kind of tree in the surrounding forest, and I intervened in the struggle of "let the best tree win" and decided that the best tree here would be sugar maples. They now make a gorgeous sight, and my successors will have an option for income next to the residence.

Starting out on a mid-March morning, I had collected a bucketful of sap by dusk. I poured the sap into the evaporator over the fire outside my cabin and boiled it until the flame went out and only six inches of fluid remained. The sap continued to run from the trees into the buckets until an early-morning freeze, when a couple of hours later, I had collected another bucket and a half of fresh sap. Air temperatures read at just 3°F above freezing, and I got the fire up to speed and collected another batch of sap.

The maples continued dripping and didn't stop until the cold night. They don't just have a day versus night sap flow, although it would seem so from the usual sunshine and warming during the day versus freezing at night. It is a good thing to know the trees' habits, which could mean much to the animals that depend on the sap for their lives, especially the spring's first flying insect, a signal of accelerated warming and an end to the long hard winter.

MOST WINTER MOTHS are not used to our sap buckets and often drown in them. The first one I found could have been mistaken for a half-inch piece of broken twig or bark floating in my sap bucket at dawn. Its legs, wings, and antennae were closely pressed to its gray-brown body. It seemed dead until it moved its legs, and I picked it up. It had likely flown into the bucket the previous evening before temperatures dropped below freezing. It was an otherwise common owlet moth (family Noctuidae), but this one was a rare exception among this group of hundreds of species. In most moths only their eggs or pupae and occasionally the larvae have evolved the physiology to survive freezing, but these survive winter under the leaves on the forest floor.

I hadn't known where these winter moths hibernated, but one fall I caught a lot of them after dark using diluted maple syrup smeared onto a tree trunk. I released them into an outdoor screened cage. The next day I found them under the leaves on the ground. But now the ground was still mostly under several feet of densely packed snow. I concluded that *this* individual moth in the bucket must have flown here in near-freezing temperatures, guided by the scent of sap to suck up its first (tiny) bit of sugar fuel. Then, these moths' amazing ability of shivering had raised its body temperature to get ready for flight at night. Such heating up is an amazing feat for so small an animal. Studies have shown that when its pelage-like insulation on the thorax is magnified, it could pass for that of a mouse.

THE NEW EARLY moth in a bucket was just one more attraction of being out in nature for extended periods of time, where contact leads to one thing and then on to another that could never be anticipated. Similarly, observing the owlet moths led to another surprise for me, found while I was watching (mainly) ravens at their food caching in a large aviary surrounded by sugar maple trees. Aside from the fall-flying hot-blooded moths, I saw a red squirrel that I would not have noticed except for my having been a near captive, hidden in the sugaring shack to follow an experiment on ravens in the aviary and having come upon the moths. I'd been sitting there each day for hours after having checked the sap buckets, watching the ravens. I happened to see a red squirrel every day, leading to an even more exciting story: The squirrel, it was soon apparent after a few days, had a "trapline" of nicks bitten *into* sugar maple twigs and traveled to visit them along a series of trees, visiting the *same* young maples and the sap licks at intervals of one day to the next. Its single deep bites into a twig issued sap that ran down and later evaporated to leave syrup, not only taken by the squirrel by day, but then also the moths at dusk.

The winter geometer moths (family Geometridae), which sail rather than have powered flight, had all died soon after mating and laying eggs. But these hot-blooded *owlet* moths crawl under the fallen leaves and go into an all-winter torpor, like woodchucks and jumping mice, and then lay their eggs in spring as soon as the sap runs.

Meanwhile, the woodcock had been waiting for the first patch of open ground on the field as his landing pad in between sky dances—so high in the sky that he was barely visible. I await his arrival every spring and rejoice. His is, to me, the sweetest music I have ever heard, and I have listened to him since I was a teen on our farm, where I set a tent near the blooming willow where he fluttered down on his shooting-star descent.

These memories fold, one into another, making a fabric like the ecosystem, where each affects the other in a never-ending chain of relationships. In their whole there is beauty, and beauty is nothing more and nothing less than worth. Each can be vastly different from one to another. The maple trees' worth was now shown, and I love the grove I created.

AFTER FREEING THE moth, I returned to maple sugaring. The outside temperature with the rising sun rose quickly to a cozy-seeming 43°F and produced a strong sap run. I was kept busy bringing the now dried wood that I had collected last year into the shed—splitting it and feeding the fire to sustain a billowing white steam cloud rising up above the froth of the boiling sap in the 16-by-16-inch-wide and foot-deep boiling pan. The steam rose several yards before vanishing into the dry air, looking like a veil of pale blue smoke, wafting off the fire and dissipating into the distance. Where there is worth there is substance. And substance itself has its own beauty if we know it. Otherwise, we don't see it either.

The sap-to-syrup transformation made by the heat comes from the energy released from the wood burned of the other trees I'd felled, their stored energy having been made by nuclear reactions in the sun that had traveled here at the speed of light, to be captured by the leaves, and in the process taking carbon dioxide molecules out of the air to make a six-carbon molecule as the raw material for stitching these molecules together to make wood. No artificial solar collector is as attractive, has as many uses available to so many animals, or can come close to the efficiency and beauty that nature provides.

The sap, by the stimulus of heat activating the trees' physiology, runs up the trunks to transport the sugar that had been made from carbon the previous year. That stored energy of the carbon-carbon links, along with the carbon itself, will be up in the treetops in a few weeks, to be used to construct leaves—the world's most amazing solar panels—to collect more carbon again, for growing even taller trees.

But energy stored in sugar can't be all that there is in this sap. When concentrated into syrup, it has a unique and pleasant taste that is derived from much more than sugar. It contains all the nutrients necessary to make the leaves that feed the caterpillars, which then grow and metamorphose into moths and butterflies, which are then fed to many birds. Mainly that synthesis requires proteins, so the sap must contain amino acids, the building blocks, plus vitamins, minerals, and everything else needed to make an animal from a plant. If leaves can grow caterpillars, which are in theory (and often in practice) suitable healthful food for birds, then sap likely contains other nutrients besides sugar for us humans. We like the taste, and that alone is a sign of the body's approval.

It has been a long time since I have been hungry—decades— but I still know what hunger is. If I *were* hungry, I'd eat caterpillars—at least the green ones that try to hide, although I'd shun all that are in flashy colorful garb, for they would contain the spines and toxins to protect themselves from being eaten by birds, the same toxins that they had likely obtained from the leaves the plant had produced to protect itself from animals that might browse them for their food.

THE THREE QUARTS of syrup I produced from my sixteen taps is enough to last a long time. So here I am, sitting comfortably on the stump cut with a chain saw, as I watch and hear the roil of boiling sap, thinking how in 1980 I probably sat at this same fireplace of several strategically placed flat rocks and dreamt of this. I look at the sugar maple trees that some three decades earlier were broom-pole saplings, among a brush thicket of pine, white ash, paper birch, cherry, beech, spruce, fir, quaking aspen, and old dying apple trees, all vying to overtake each other in what had once been a cow pasture and then an apple orchard. As I write this, in 2024, there is now a grove of fifty-foot-tall maple trees (where there was not one maple before) among several deliberately left pine, red oak, paper birch, white ash, beech, and baby American chestnut trees, thriving in all directions.

I return in my mind to that earlier time by counting the trees' growth rings, as revealed by my chain saw. I had recently done some tree thinning where once again the maple trees were crowding each other and reducing the growth ring widths to a fraction of an inch. I felled trees that were close together to have the wood dry for fuel through the summer and fall. I love big trees but need fire year-round.

The date of 1980 was clearly visible in the *then* mere fraction of an inch growth rings suddenly released and expanding to several times wider in subsequent years. The trees now shot up and out, thickening to ten inches, which calculates to a volume increase of about forty-five times.

My trees still growing in the forest now average about a thirty-inch circumference breast high versus fifty-five inches for several I planted in the open clearing. And now, in some places in the grove, their seedlings covering the ground weave the stitch of a carpet, only inches apart. One in millions of them will grow tall and thick and become the homes of woodpeckers, nuthatches, chickadees—overnighting places for surviving winter nights. Not just for one species, but many, and that includes me.

I'll take some trees to heat my house and cook my meals with, instead of using propane pumped from the ground to release carbon dioxide that was sequestered millions of years ago and transported here from perhaps a thousand miles away, out of sight of our eyes. My food and my heat will come mostly from what is already here and has been circulating within a system where every part is not *apart* but a *part* of everything else, in a unity of interrelationships. The brush field has become a source of firewood and will be a potential source of hardwood logs. It has already allowed what I had dreamed of—sugaring in my lifetime. The forest has poured in, like sap into a bucket.

In sugaring time, that sap counts not just for me. The resident yellow-bellied sapsuckers will be back any day now, and I'm often excited by unexpected surprises, such as when the pair nested in a cavity they hammered into a dead branch stub of an old sugar maple that afforded me a ringside seat (literally) of their nesting cycle. But still, being with "my" trees for years, I was long surprised one recent spring by not seeing these sapsuckers tapping the sugar maples—or any maples. How could I miss what they are famous for?

The fact is they didn't pass up sugar maples, but only recently did I finally notice. I had been distracted looking at their huge, conspicuous sap-lick stations on birch trees, which often, if not usually, end up killing the trees, so I had not seen them sugaring on maple trees until it was revealed to me on the large sugar maple directly next to the outhouse. I was there parked in leisure when I saw a male sapsucker near a thin streak of sap running down the tree. Its source was a tiny hole through the bark.

"So what?" one may think. But from what had come before, this was a big deal. It concerned the common red squirrel, *Tamiasciurus hudsonicus.*

Thirty years earlier I had been alerted to the sugar maple sap story of red squirrels after discovering that they make sap taps in sugar maples and lap maple *syrup*, not just using sap as a source of water. (Why would they, with all that snow, which I now use, too?) The squirrels were taking advantage of natural temperature changes of night and day. During cold nights the air holds little moisture, but when the air warms up in the daytime from the sun, it can hold a lot. The dramatic difference in the air's uptake of moisture depending on its temperature means that it sucks up water like a sponge when the temperature goes from low to high, causing evaporation if a large surface area is provided low humidity.

The red squirrels routinely take advantage of this phenomenon by biting into the thin bark of young sugar maple twigs, sending the sap running down in long streaks so that within a day of their being made, the surface area expands and the sap becomes concentrated. (I have licked them and tasted the sweet at the tip of the tongue.) The squirrels' "trapline" of feeding stations which they then visit regularly in the daytime. The process is much like our own process of sugaring, except that we work with large volumes and facilitate the evaporation by applied heat rather than the natural diurnal cycle of temperature change.

Still, I still hadn't yet "gotten" all that was going on; I could not dismiss that the squirrels might be doing something more. I tried to duplicate what they did by nicking the bark of twigs to mimic their taps, but I got no sap! Why was that? In retrospect, I was not considering the system from the trees' perspective. I should have known that the sap comes from the xylem tubes—the tubes that conduct the fluid upward. These are in the wood as the tree is sending nutrients up in the vehicle of water, from the roots where the sugar had been stored over the winter to now feed the buds for flower, twig, and leaf growth in the flush of early spring.

My simplest experiment of trying to mimic the red squirrels' behavior and failing gave me insights into other sapsucker behavior that eventually led to solving the puzzle. The hint: Sapsuckers "never" kill any maple trees in the forest here, but they routinely killed mature *birch trees*. Why? It is because they use a different technique on maples to get the same if not more sap.

Although the sapsuckers return north from migration and tap sugar maples long before any tree leaves open, they generally don't tap birch until about two months later. And what do they do? They then tap the *phloem* sap—that which flows *down* in the tubes of the inner bark once the leaves are producing nutrients. To access *that* source, the sapsuckers remove a fraction-of-an-inch piece of bark, but only *down to* the wood, not into it as in maple. Sap coming down flows over the bared wound at first, but the tree defends itself by shutting off that flow over that surface, and the sap then flows around the wound. The sapsucker removes bark above or to the side to again intercept the flow. This begins a game of tree-versus-sapsucker, where one is always trying to stay ahead of the other. The sapsucker feasts on the same tree all summer long and then again for the next year or so, ever more enlarging the tree wound until eventually the birch tree is girdled by sap taps and dies.

The sapsucker, meanwhile, feeds not only from the sap, but also from the by-then numerous insects that come to it, so a sapsucker gets a "complete" diet of sugar for energy as well as sufficient protein for growth and reproduction. At the same time, other animals partake of the largess resulting from the sapsuckers' work as well. The visually most prominent of these beneficiaries where I am are the ruby-throated hummingbirds, who because of the woodpecker can live in the Northern Forest, traveling to it all the way from South and Central America. The local dining sapsucker-dependent crowd also commonly incudes the predatory white-faced hornets, as well as butterflies and red squirrels in the daytime and northern flying squirrels and moths at night.

The yellow-bellied sapsuckers' two quite different harvesting strategies in the Northern Forest are supplemented by a third that has the same effect of getting sap and protein. I have had the good fortune to observe this strategy from up close directly in front of my desk through my cabin window. A large birch tree there, one like any other, has only one obvious difference—it is infested with plant lice, more commonly called aphids, which insert their mouthparts into the trees' leaves and young shoots to take in phloem sap. Hardly moving at all, they have little need for food calories. Instead, they need mostly amino acids to build protein for growth and egg production. It takes a lot of plant fluid to get enough amino acids, and aphids have to *excrete* (by their anus) much water to retain a concentrate of the amino acid protein building blocks for growth and reproduction. Ants have evolved much of the same system as ours of domesticating cattle for milk production; normally predacious, they literally herd the aphids and "milk" them by collecting their sweet excess, though from their anal secretions, not teats. Every summer I see several ant trails with constant traffic up and down the white birch by my window. Half of the ants on any one trail are running up the tree, the other down—mirroring xylem and phloem—back and forth between loading up with aphids at the top of the tree and unloading in their nest below ground.

Sapsuckers have learned that many of these ants are bloated blobs of sweets packaged in protein and park at a convenient spot on the tree trunk and partake of the feast. It does not require much skill to pick off ants, but I adopted one sapsucker that soon got steak instead. It had been a fledgling that apparently had not been able to "make it" when I picked it up off a dirt road. It was at first too weak to fly, and I took it home to the cabin, as I am a poor aphid picker. It enjoyed the steak and soon trusted me enough to take the meat from my mouth when I leaned against the tree it perched on by the door. Soon after it gained the strength to fly. It began to recognize my voice and learned to come to me out of the woods when called . . . until one day it came no more. Perhaps it had discovered sweetened ants.

The following spring, a yellow-bellied sapsucker returned at maple sugaring time. It arrived long before the tree by the door had any leaves—or ants. I wished it were the same bird, but there was no way to know.

Three

The Unexpected Is Usually Most Interesting by Its Contrasts

Emotions are a basic mechanism. We are endowed with many of them at birth. Like other physiological mechanisms, these are shared among species and can be assumed to be present in others, just as we may assume every vertebrate animal has a heart, a brain, lungs, liver, and alimentary canal. We might instead try to see what a swallow sees, and how its specific needs and circumstances are similar to or different from ours. We can also, through empathy, come to understand the feelings of other species, but this empathy must be based on knowledge.

WHITE FEATHERS, 2020

THE SNOW WAS STILL DEEP; IT WAS HARD TO IMAGine spring. When I awoke one morning, the wood frogs (*Rana sylvatica*) had finished their concert in the nearby pool, and the spring peepers were still singing at full volume. Robins and eastern phoebes were nesting under my roof overhang, and a pair of black-capped chickadees had taken over one of the four swallow boxes I provided; another that had been home to several deer mice was now available for occupancy.

Most birds' spring procedure is to hurry and build a nest, lay their eggs, incubate them, and then, when the young hatch, care for them until they become independent. Tree swallows (*Tachyci-*

neta bicolor) add another step. I had previously observed and pondered why these blue-green, gray-brown, and white birds line their nests with white feathers. I knew of no others that did the same, yet in my observations of these birds for ten consecutive nesting seasons, I had not found the answer to their apparent white feather obsession, despite tests and comparisons. Nevertheless, ten years seemed enough to record the adventure, and so eventually I wrote a book about it, but was now tempted to open the topic for another look.

Swallows are conspicuous and famous for their gracefulness of flight. Many species are also famed for their perfection in making nests from mud. This striking and epochal innovation, like the ancient Romans' use of cement, opened new home options for them. It allowed some species to nest on sheer cliffs and take up residence inside open doors of barns, sheds, and garages. However, tree swallows never pick up mud, they do not construct such nest frames, nor do they dig them into sandbanks, like bank swallows (*Riparia riparia*) do, nor can they excavate cavities into wood like woodpeckers. Instead, they normally nest in abandoned woodpecker nest holes.

That's not enough for swallows, who need their homes associated with open space, which in the North Woods is most available in bogs created by beavers' activity of both felling trees and drowning the rest by their ponds created by dams. Availability of both tree holes for nests and open sky for catching flying insects, provided by beavers and people, allows these swallows to raise their young far north, then spend much of their lives farther south, all the way into Central America. Returning north in early May to their ready-made nest sites, they get their offspring flight-ready by the first of July, to begin their return to the southern climes, having reduced their entire sojourn in the north into less than two months. True lovers of the North Woods they are not. They like open space and take advantage of cavities found there for one thing only: reproduction.

Most tree swallows I get to know nest in a human-made bird box, from which they have access to human-made field/pasture/lawn space. Not surprisingly, they have therefore, by coming close when we want them, become—like lab rats—the ideal study animals for researchers, as they can easily be on hand. This species is especially famous for apparent record frequency of extra-pair copulation (EPC), demonstrated from comparisons of the DNA between different members of the presumably same clutch of young. From experimental setups to "test" this hypothesis, it has *seemingly* been "proven," although these females may sometimes drop an egg into others' nests in an artificial nesting area, such as identical nest boxes uniformly close together on a mowed lawn. Their aboriginal home in the wild is likely a beaver bog, where each potential nest hole is necessarily in a different tree, at a different height, and with different directions of entrance holes, as well as different surroundings at any nest hole. There are in the wild *never* rows of nest sites of identical structure, evenly spaced one beside the other in a uniform lawn. As an analogy, I would personally find it difficult to locate a specific apartment in a housing complex in the city. We reduce such potential confusion by deliberately attaching signs on streets, houses, and doors.

Having spent ten consecutive years trying to find out why tree swallows lined their nests with white feathers, I had merely suggested that the white feathers in a nest may possibly serve as an "occupied" sign, such as the "No trespassing" notices people post on their driveways.

BY MAY 6, 2023, all the sugar maple trees of the forest surrounding my clearing were beautiful in their golden yellow flower tassels, and no leaves were yet in sight. It was a gorgeous day of blue sky, and the local male phoebe, who was still without a mate, was calling crazily. I was outside enjoying the morning when I suddenly stopped in my tracks, hearing a sweet gurgling intermingled with a tinkling sound: tree swallows!

To my not too great surprise, a pair of tree swallows were investigating the cement nest box with the removable panel I'd recently set out in my clearing, and they had at once devoted their attention to it, and mine to them. The swallows' eagerness reflected a chronic housing shortage, for in the context of the usual tree swallow real estate values, it is all about location, location, location. I was happy to finally see them back and to see their enthusiasm, which ignited mine for what they might tell me this time. I had, as usual, no agenda: my standard on which to recognize the new.

One of the pair was perched at the box entrance peeking in, and the other was circling overhead, flying swiftly all around, and making the swallows' pretty tinkling calls. The pair was expressing their enthusiasm, and I knew I'd now have *real* entertainment for at least a month. And by "real" I mean something without any "make believe."

The next dawn, May 7, the newly arrived swallows' soft, sweet liquid chittering resumed as they circled high above the clearing. The male, garbed in metallic shiny blue above and snow-white below, was clearly distinguishable from the female with her brownish tinge. He perched on the box and repeated a two-note refrain. She flew around but to my surprise several times swooped down and landed on the ground in the garden to pick up a piece of grass and then fly straight back and dive into the nest box with it. He meanwhile did not budge from his perch, the top of the pole holding the cement box.

On the next day she again circled over and around in the clearing and the garden as before, to dive down onto the ground to pick up more pieces of dry grass and circle back and swoop into the beginning nest, one trip right after another, for a half hour. Then both swallows circled high and flew away. In three days, the nest cup was fully formed and seemed complete except for feathers. In the meantime, however, a third swallow, a female, had arrived, but the resident female always chased her off. The male, meanwhile, continued not to budge from his perch at the nest box. On May 16, there were again three swallows in the air, but as on every morning, the male remained perched in the vicinity of the nest box in the closest tree, giving to me, and I suspect to his original mate, pleasant-sounding two-note calls.

My notes span many pages of all sorts of other spring happenings, but those of the swallows grew repetitive from their arrival ten days earlier. The nest remained unchanged. It looked like a deep cup with solid sides of dead grass straws neatly arranged in a circle. Both the nest box and the sky over the field were within my easy viewing.

Then I suddenly saw them aggressively chasing a third swallow high in the sky, swirling all over and swiftly flying back and forth. And then they were gone. (There were four other nest boxes available and prominently visible the whole time, but they did not approach any of them.)

It might have become boring, but I did not want to miss anything, as the unexpected is usually the most interesting by its contrast. I would of course like to make discoveries, but more than that I was interested in what the swallows' feelings were, to get an idea what their world is like, to then perhaps be poised to discover something. And so, along the sidelines, I watched a pair of blue-birds that were excited at one of the other boxes, while a gold-finch sang just above me in the maple tree, in such a soft whisper as to be barely audible. Goldfinches' nesting season is not until August, long after the swallows have flown south, to time their young for feeding them the then-available thistle seed crop. So, the finch was not singing to advertise himself, but because he was feeling good at my bird feeder with lots of black sunflower seeds. A male purple finch loudly chattered while chasing a female, who continually evaded him but still stayed in the same leafy sugar maple tree. I had no clue what was going on, as they were hidden most of the time, unlike the swallows so prominent in the open sky and easily visible when on a tree and perched at the top.

Finally, May 19, the swallows exhibited a sudden huge switch. I was up at dawn as usual to check their nest box to see if they possibly overnighted there or might have laid an egg. The box was still empty, a beautiful nest cup of grass strands folded smoothly into a circle, but still without even one feather. At 5:30 a.m. a single swallow flew extremely high, circling, and a half hour later, when the first sunrays lit the tree leaves, the male landed as usual on the tip of the pole holding the nest box. However, this time he left his post after just four minutes to zoom into the nest. Was he checking its contents? If so, then why, and why now? He had so far not lifted a straw, and since having long expected an egg, I waited to check until he left the box.

It still held no egg.

He again perched on the pole and again went into the nest box and again came out quickly, and *she* then entered it, too, but came right back out as well. This was odd behavior, and I stayed keeping watch, as during the next hour they *both* continued to repeat their visits into their nest box without carrying anything, then to fly up into the top of the nearby black cherry tree, where they finally did it: mating.

On each flight to the top of the cherry tree, he fluttered up and down on her to mate, performing the typical bird cloacal kiss, one after another. After a few minutes he did it again. And then again still . . . and when at 7:30 a.m. they finally quit, I checked the nest box: It had not changed; still no egg and not a single feather.

I was out near dawn on the next day, May 20, and found the male perched as usual directly above the nest box. However, another that I could not identify but at first presumed to be his mate, was circling in the sky when a *third* joined the circling bird. Meanwhile, he continued to stay perched near the nest site. Then one of the two in flight flew down to the nest box, where she hung at the entrance looking in as the male next to it continued his usual chortle. But then came a sudden switch as *another* female (by her duller color) grappled with the nest owner, and wildly fluttering they fell into the weeds just below the nest. They tangled fiercely for several minutes at a time. Both females were oblivious to me even as they fought almost directly by my feet, while he, meanwhile, stayed near the nest entrance, although once in a while fluttered down to the two females' fight on and in the ground vegetation that included low-bush blueberry. He did not interfere physically, but it would have been difficult, since the two were entangled with each other as well as with and in the vegetation.

This was the most vicious and the longest bird fight I had ever seen, certainly more gripping than watching to see who could kick a ball between two posts. But this was no game; it was for real. Something was at stake. At times, the swallows untangled for over a minute, separated, and then went at it again. Again and again after they untangled, one would fly to the nest box entrance as if to block it but did not enter. The fight continued for about *an hour*, when the original female finally landed on the nearby apple tree, the pair's favorite perching place. Her mate then flew over to her and made two brief perfunctory mating attempts that were not well received, and he immediately returned to his usual perch on top of the pole holding the nest box.

During the tussles, neither of the two females had entered the nest box, but I don't think it was incidental that *now* was precisely the time for egg laying to start, since the first egg appeared in that nest—the morning after the battle.

At early dawn of May 23, the nest still contained only one egg and not a single feather.

Both birds were always present at daybreak, the male perching on top of the pole holding the nest box or now, more often, on the nearby apple tree with bare dead branches. Subsequently, in the next days, the female entered the nest box early in the morning, before *both* then left for much of the day, but returned several times to repeat their apparent guarding. The third swallow was gone. And the nest still had no feathers.

Could their many eggless days have been because they were unable to find feathers? If so, why had the swallows in previous years always found them?

My hunch is that they could not have found them in the tree canopy of the continuous forest in all directions as the nearest beaver bog had been drained. Were there not geese nearby? Were there no feathers at all to be found? With that question

I procured chicken feathers of different colors, shapes, and sizes from my friends, Betty and Ted Simanek, who had often provided me with chicken eggs. I sprinkled a dozen or so of these various feathers around the field by the nest box. The response was unexpectedly instant and vigorous, as the male perched on the top of the pole holding the nest box chortled endless renditions of his liquid-sounding refrains. The female immediately started fetching the feathers, and without a break made trip after trip picking up a single feather each time and making a beeline to the nest. While she was busy, he meanwhile didn't lift a feather, just like he hadn't picked up a piece of grass. But in less than a half hour the nest was transformed, although the feathers were not all white. The long ones with a bend were preferred and placed with their curled tops providing a partial cover over the nest mold. She had rejected the small white fuzzy ones, so choice was likely not all about color.

After this several-minute-long feather-fetching stint, neither brought in more feathers, even though I still made them available during subsequent weeks. He now left the pole, and they perched next to each other on their then already highly favored dry twig of the old apple tree, at a fifty-yard distance from the nest. But now he stayed silent. They left at 9:00 a.m. As usual, he hadn't lifted a feather, but the nest was feathered out with all the feathers it could contain, although so far it still contained only one egg.

Dropping an egg into another's nest is a well-known behavior of birds and is the sole strategy of parenting in some cuckoos and in cowbirds, where parasitizing is practiced only on other species, since they've given it up for themselves. In the resulting wars of evolution by one species against the other, the parasitizing option evolved the "strategy" of mimicking the eggs of the host in coloration so as to reduce the likelihood of the host's detection of the parasite egg. That's where the variety of design and the beauty of birds' eggs come from. However, many birds also parasitize the nests of individuals of their *own* species, where the egg color already matches that of the hosts closely and color cannot serve as the sole cue to detect a foreign egg. The parents removing a foreign egg would then be a risky option.

No swallow or other bird had been near to observe when on June 3 I inserted a tree swallow egg into the couple's nest of five eggs (from one of a group of boxes I had once watched years ago at a clearing by a lake). I painted this swallow egg with spots of reddish brown to be sure it would be identified. I did not see the female after that, but didn't take much notice because the male was near as routinely as before. He was on his pole by the box every day, and I assumed she was inside, but I didn't want to be an agent in her potentially leaving, so I didn't open the box to look in. Finally, by June 11, I climbed a chestnut tree and sat on a limb to observe from a distance. Once when he had left, I quickly descended the tree and went to take a look: She was not on the nest, and it still contained the egg I had inserted. However, instead of it being at the back of the clutch, the extra one was now at the *front*. It had been moved. It could not likely have been *removed* from the nest, since swallows do not have bills for pecking into or holding an egg. They could, however, roll an egg toward the entrance, but not up the wall of the hole and then up and out. Noticing and dealing with foreign eggs is, however, on the swallows' evolved behavioral agenda if caring for extra young is a serious enough cost, as I suspected from the earlier fights when the lone foreign female tried to enter the nest at precisely when egg laying was to start. But where were they?

By the next afternoon I still had not seen the female, but the male was back on his perch by the nest. This time, he remained silent for hours. It was so unusual; something was up, and I forced myself to keep watching from my tree perch, waiting for something to happen. Finally, as I was about to give up, he moved his head in quick jerky motions and then dropped down to the nest box entrance. But instead of entering like "always," this time he just stuck his head in and out and then took off, making one quick call. I'm sure he knew beforehand that she was not there the whole time, because there had been no vocal exchange whatsoever, and he now flew off without a backward look. During those three hours he had sat there alone and waited and likely knew she was gone and would not be back.

I did not see him again, though as before I habitually looked for the pair. The nest was abandoned. Apparently, the newly inserted foreign swallow egg had indeed spooked the female. She alone had made this nest. She alone responded to the intruder and apparently also to the extra egg. On average, those who did not respond with vigor were cuckolded. The cuckolding, as one parenting strategy in this species, had evolved because its main nesting limitation is the rarity of appropriate nest sites in the Northern Forest.

I still didn't know if the seemingly costly behavior of lining their nests with white feathers is a possible cuckolding defense. However, the results now made me almost accept my hypothesis, because here there were *two* empty nest boxes available, yet the second apparently lone female risked and endured a pounding by the nest-owning one to try to enter the one nest, precisely the one that was ready for the owners to deposit their clutch. Entering the second nest box would have cost the second female nothing, except the egg would not have had a chance to fledge an offspring. But of course, she did not have a mate, so this *potential* option was not possible.

White feathers are indeed a conspicuous sign that the nest cavity is taken. The first egg in likely signifies priority, and a nest containing feathers is likely to contain one or more eggs. A potential cuckold risks losing her own egg if the nest owners sense its actual or likely presence. Either could lose or win, depending on timing and/or resolve.

These swallows are one of the most tolerant of birds to each other: After nesting they join up into groups of thousands, and at overwintering sites in the south they roost together in millions. Nest guarding, however, is intense. Neither of this pair of swallows dive-bombed me as they might have and as others have done routinely and vigorously, like kamikaze fighters on a mission, coming within inches of my head.

The animosity the swallow pair had expressed to the "new" female that had tried to enter their nest on *precisely* the day before the first egg appeared, not to mention the pummeling the female nest owner meted out to her rival just then, was likely based on expectations of what the second female was up to, and that was unlikely to be anything else than to drop in an egg because she had not been accompanied by a mate.

There is, however, another hypothesis on the possible adaptive use of white feathers. Researchers in Norway had recently observed the use of white feathers in several European bird species, including tree swallows. They suggested that to potential nest parasites, the white feathers could be a sign of nearby predation—a red flag that signals a predator residing in the vicinity. I'm skeptical!

Yet this experience, along with so many others, convinced me that the details matter, as threads make cloth one stitch at a time, as one paint stroke, one word, one sighting following another leads to a goal. And the best of any destination or adventure is not known but found by facts as tracks into the unknown. Understanding and empathy are never far apart.

Part II

Becoming

Four

Foresight, Distant Origins, and Imprints of Home

*No nonroutine behavior is without risk, but almost any change can
under appropriate circumstances result in improvement and cannot
be anticipated.*

RACING THE CLOCK, 2021

I HAVE BEEN LUCKY TO HAVE TREE SWALLOWS DANCING right at my doorstep, like some people have pets. Canada geese are not far behind in availability, because they are social animals that, like dogs, have a strong tendency to bond with family and vice versa. We come to understand them, and they us. One can easily appreciate how and why they became domesticated, just as other herd animals did, namely, horses, cows, sheep, goats, chickens, ducks, guinea fowl, elephants, donkeys, and turkeys. They are all genetically programmed to associate with others of similar bents to social behavior and context, as are (especially) wolves to a pack and thus dogs to the humans they grow up with.

Yet geese are not always welcome by everyone, because fresh green grass is their favorite food, and once they find a good patch they return, leaving much behind that is not desired by any host with a goal of not only keeping grass very short and very green but also unfertilized. Such habitat is rare in the woods, except where the trees have been removed, which, as with the swallows, was undoubtedly for millennia associated with the beaver presence. As far as the geese are concerned, we are as convenient as beavers, whose lodges they favor as prime nesting places. As an added bonus to cutting trees, building even bigger dams, and creating ponds, we humans repel predators. So, the geese are thriving like never before and would take over golf courses everywhere if only they provided a pool at every other hole. Geese are predisposed to become our coinhabitants as friends and neighbors. And in my case, they had been close associates as perhaps puppies are to kids, although goslings are even fuzzier, cuter, and more loyal followers.

The freshly hatched young of geese, as well as those of grouse, turkeys, ducks, cranes, and sandpipers, to name a few, leave the nest right after emerging and stay with their parents in a rapid learning called imprinting. Forty-five years ago, when I lived in Hinesburg, Vermont, to teach at the university, I parented Peep, a Canada goose, from the day she hatched from the egg as a tiny yellow fluffball. According to theory, she should have been imprinted on me—that is, to consider me a model of the species and so to eventually, when she grew up, consider me the proper model to seek for a mate.

Peep didn't, although she had indeed followed me slavishly, as she would her parents, because I'd been acting as a parent for her. By autumn, she got excited when I started my truck, also as if imprinted on it, and she would even fly alongside when I drove down a back road. That behavior, though, was not by imprinting, but by a genetically innate response to specific stimuli. The sound of the motor and the size of the moving truck had apparently triggered the innate response to migrate with the flock that would normally contain the family. In this case that was me.

However, later that fall she finally did leave with another goose, after the two had repeatedly come to my door and not found me there. I did not expect to ever see Peep again, since she had found a mate more suitable than me.

It was a huge surprise when the following spring a pair of geese showed up on our lawn next to our beaver bog in Hinesburg. One of them, I presumed the gander, stood stock still, seemingly in alarm, with his head held as high as is possible by his long-stretched neck. The other, I presumed his mate, was relaxed and lazily walking around on the lawn, showing no fear or care, as one might expect of a creature coming to a familiar place. She now wore a metal ring on one leg. It turned out she had, in the interim, been banded in a Vermont Department of Fish and Game roundup of geese as they gather in groups of hundreds when they lose their flight feathers in late summer to grow new ones for the fall migration.

I approached the pair, and she, instead of retreating, casually walked up to me while her gander held back with his head still and ever higher. I offered her food, and she had no more reservation coming to me than to him. She had returned to her place of birth, brought along a mate, and perhaps would stay to nest.

Peep built a nest among the sedge tussocks in the bog adjacent to the lawn, and she knew me as I knew her. I saw the nest from a high tree at the pond edge and went to that nest when she was incubating. I knelt beside it and talked to her. I noticed her leg band as she very slowly stood up. As she allowed me to pull an egg from under her to examine it, she remained nonchalant, and so did he, whereas at other nests the pair threatens anyone that comes close to them. *Did she remember me?* I think so, as she told in gestures such as reaching down and casually toying with a stray feather at the nest's edge. I knew from prior experience what wild ganders do in such situations when strangers near their nest: They erupt in violent and indeed frightening displays of aggression. But this gander, her mate, stood stock still about twenty yards distant with head held high. He saw how *she* welcomed me, and he believed her. It was as if her gestures were saying, "He's okay, don't worry." The gander understood, craned his neck up high, and stared!

Science does not get much better than this, but I didn't write a research report in an ornithology journal on the ramifications of imprinting of *Branta canadensis*, because the results were *too* obvious to make tests worth the while.

IN THE YEARS since, I have missed the geese. My clearing in the Maine woods is now a poor place for them, but I was pleased to see a pair of "totally" wild ones taking a shine to an artificial pond built at the edge of my hometown here. Mr. Procter the elder, who dug the pond years ago, had left an island in it that inadvertently became the perfect replica of a beaver lodge for a pair of Canada geese. Year after year the pair returns, and for all intents and purposes they now appear in behavior indistinguishable from domestic geese. They graze on the lawn directly by the house occupied by *Homo sapiens*—the Procter family. The Procter lawn surrounds the pond and the geese feed all over it from spring to fall, favoring the fresh often-mowed grass. Nonbreeder geese from the lake two miles away sometimes take the cue and come to peacefully join the resident pair, who in spring fight viciously for the single nesting place, the tiny island in the pond. Directly at the edge of the pond and the house is a highway, and I suspect strangers driving by would assume that the geese are domestic. They show no fear, although they do waddle off if someone comes to a stop to stare or photograph them. As I write now in late October, a flock of about forty have joined them, and they are within ten yards of the busy highway and two miles of my doorway.

The resident pair at the Procters' pond have up to six young per year, but in 2023 only one of the clutch survived, either because of an attack by an otter (one had been spotted locally) or because the nest got flooded from excessive rain. Other geese are now routinely tolerated after nesting time, and they graze on the Procter family's well-mowed lawn that always has fresh grass as they fatten up before migrating. I suspect the plentiful greens allow them to stay, and they do stay even as others pass through.

Geese not only fatten up and grow new flight feathers in the fall to prepare to migrate, but must also come to a consensus *about precisely when* as a group to leave the Northern Forest to fly south, to be able to graze, most likely on other lawns nowadays. Migrating by flying in a V saves energy, which requires coming to a consensus on departure and then aligning in flight among a group of cooperating individuals.

Last year as I drove up the Procters' driveway for a visit, I approached the pair with their one remaining gosling. The gander lowered his head, took several steps toward me, and hissed. He was not afraid of me, nor I of him, and I left with a smile, thinking of Peep, and wishing these (to me) unnamed ones well in taking to the air, then on some cue by one or more taking to the sky, forming a V, and flying to a likely predetermined location— perhaps Chicago—for the winter.

The pair returned again this spring as soon as the snow melted and ice was gone, raising four young as usual. Most years they'd have left by mid-September. However, this year they are still all here at the end of October.

I had never thought of the geese as overly exciting, as I see them "all the time" now, but I never tire of them. I don't expect much because of their almost boring tranquility and constant presence. All that changed as I recorded in my daily diary of October 13, 2024:

Oh! My God! What an experience to (near) finish of the day (at my cabin on top of the hill) starting with the brightest red dawn all year. It wasn't planned (most aren't—if they were they would never be a surprise and would be a disappointment). I'd just finished off the afternoon working on my woodpile (there can never be enough), when my chainsaw conked out, so I went with the ax on to the lighter stuff that's good for kindling at dawn. But this was at 2:45 PM. The sky was clouding up pretty fast, after a lot of sun, and I got back inside to finish off the day to see what would happen next. It was so very quiet. No wind. No sun. A solid gray all around. It seemed "dead" except for the birds at the feeder—including the male purple finch, when suddenly I heard . . . could it be? Canada geese? Yes, it sure was, and it sounded like a big but distant crowd.

I bounded outside and scanned the gray sky—and saw the largest V I'd ever seen. Really! At least a hundred to each side, and they were heading precisely southwest. They were gabbling nonstop and were certainly too high up to land here. There was no sight in the sky visible to me, no sun, no moon, no variation in the high cloud cover. A solid "blanket" of cloud. Birds orient by the sun, moon, and stars. There was nothing. Where had these geese been? Where were they flying to in the hugest aggregation that I'd ever seen? How had they all gathered up? Where? There was not a breath of wind. And why the nonstop chatter? They could be heard at least a mile off. Does the enormous number come from collections along the way? There is so much going on that we do not know, and we likely do not understand much of what we cannot understand—what goes on in their minds.

The timing and direction of bird migrations has been one of unraveling great mysteries leading to discoveries. It would take volumes to reveal their many dimensions that invoke awe and wonder at the capacities that are far beyond our own and give life its beauty and magic. Rarely do we get a chance to see it in real time with our own eyes. The geese and the ravens were to me marvels simply because I know so *little* about them, even though they are there as neighbors, if not more, nearly constantly. Even more intriguing are those birds that are seldom seen.

A FEW YEARS ago, at the same time as the geese were leaving, I noticed a flock of about thirty redpoll (*Carduelis flammea*), tiny finches. They had to have come south from the Arctic and arrived near my cabin. I'd seen a redpoll nest in the tundra one spring while taking a month-long canoe trip down the Noatak River, in Alaska. But these tiny circumpolar birds with their bright red caps and pink-tinged breasts occasionally come south into the North Woods to pick the seeds from the then-ripe birch catkins. It is a rare treat to see them.

The redpolls stayed all winter, yielding (for me) another once-in-a-lifetime experience, as they spent much of each day in my clearing, appearing to play in the snow after feeding each morning on black sunflower seeds at my bird feeder. Of course, finches of all sorts came to the feeder during the winter, and that winter decades hence came along with the redpoll also occasional goldfinches, purple finches, evening grosbeaks, pine grosbeaks, plus the usual, "always" the black-capped chickadees, red-breasted and white-breasted nuthatches, blue jays, downy and hairy wood-peckers, golden-crowned kinglets, and brown creepers. Yet, none of the latter did what these redpolls did as a daily routine. After having fed, the redpolls, unlike any of the others, remained in the clearing and spent most of their time not in the trees, but both on and *in* the snow. Having hopped along on the snow surface, they pushed their heads into the snow, and then continuing, pushed forward in it, making grooves and tunnels. They then, a yard or so farther, popped back up and out.

The snow tunneling did seem unlikely to accomplish much of anything in the temperate climate, but I suspect it may be nec-essary and used to advantage in the treeless far north for surviv-ing severe cold and wind by snow caving all night, as the ruffed grouse do here in the North Woods at night and sometimes in the daytime. But not just for saving body heat but also for avoiding predation. On the tundra there would be no tree shelter from the wind, nor anything like tree cavities that woodpeckers, chickadees, and nuthatches can and do create for shelter in rotting wood and then use for the night. Here in the south of the redpolls' winter range, temperatures were modest, barely −20°F, not cold enough to be threatening to them, but the conditions were likely close enough to release similar behavior, and they did it for fun, not necessity as a shelter.

I doubt that a redpoll, or any other bird that builds its first nest, thinks of what it is doing. It could never in its life have had either directions or practice, in the same way that any migrator knew where it was going when it flew off over the ocean in perhaps September out of the Maine woods to and into the Amazon forest. It just felt like it, following programmed genetic instructions, guided by stimuli that are innate, like us responding to the growl of a bear. We have genetic instructions with specific responses for specific stimuli, perhaps like (but not so precise as) a spider weaving a perfect web. It is born with all the moves. The question is not so much what the animal can do routinely that it is born to do, but rather how far can its behavior take advantage of an opportunity that is different from the routine?

THE INDIVIDUAL REDPOLL flocks rarely return for a repeat performance, but one of my favorites, the eastern phoebes (*Sayornis phoebe*), come back every spring. Their arrival is like a reunion with roommates, since their nest is almost *in* my house, several yards from my upstairs bedroom, where I can watch them from up close and hope to see what moves them.

For years, a phoebe couple has raised a clutch of young in precisely the same nest, on a cabin log under the roof by a window. This nest remains attached there over the winter due to the protection by the eaves closely above it and the solid log base below. They arrive as a couple near snow melt, when the alders and beaked hazel have been in bloom for a week and the red maples, aspen, and black cherry buds are thickening, while the red-winged blackbirds are returning. As I was finishing my maple sugaring in the spring of 2021, I was ready to watch them closely and looked forward to it in anticipation. How does the bird build its nest?

They arrived on April 8, during the warmest spring on record so far, when temperatures suddenly soared to 50°F. Mourning cloak butterflies flew, and tiny bees landed in my sap buckets. Ladybird beetles were emerging from hibernation into the cabin and gathered at the windows, searching for a way out. Then, at 8 a.m., I heard the first "fee-bees," the phoebes' excited calls alternating with loud emphatic "cheeze-reets," and saw the pair fluttering all around outside the cabin. However, a rainstorm had recently splashed onto the nest, weakened its attachment, and dislodged it so that it had fallen onto the ground. And then, after a big snowstorm and cold temperatures, the phoebes were silent . . . gone. I neither saw nor heard the pair in the nearby woods.

It was not until twenty-one days later that either they, or another pair, finally returned to nest on the precise spot under the eaves as previous years' nests. The sugar maples were then in thick yellow bloom, and the first blackflies had shown up. One of the phoebe pair immediately started rebuilding "their" nest on the old site, and on May 4, when I opened the upstairs window of the cabin to lean out, I found no eggs yet as I reached under the roof to feel into the nest. But a week later one of the pair was incubating the typical phoebe clutch of four pearly white eggs.

Dandelions had started to bloom, the pin cherry tree next to the cabin was afluff with white blossoms, and four Canada goslings had hatched from the annual nest in town and sheltered under their mom while the gander stood next to them on the lawn with his head high. The sugar maple trees had now leafed out, but not yet the ash, chestnuts, and beech. The tree swallows mated, and a pair of ruby-throated hummingbirds fed from my feeder. Meanwhile, the phoebes now seemed absent. They seldom made a peep, but they attended to their parenting routine for three weeks, busily foraging and feeding their four babies. They called only occasionally when near each other, making barely audible chirrups. But when on June 8 I finally did check the nest, I was instantly "attacked" by both members of the pair, who then ignored me, except to make their faint "cheep" calls. As expected, the babies were grown and would fledge in a week or so, and when they did (on the morning of June 16), in contrast to before, the male flew at me and bill-snapped in a rapid-fire "snap-snap-snap" as he dove at and then over me.

The pair was still near the cabin early the next morning, but then the whole family left within an hour and there was silence on the site for the next two days of June 18 and 19. However, one of the adults either remained or at times came back while its mate (probably the female) and young were out of sight and hearing. The presumed male (the sexes are difficult to distinguish) stayed perched in nearby trees by the now-empty nest, apparently guarding the nest site, as the female left with the fledglings. But why would he stay, I wondered, until June 20, when I thought I heard faint "cheeps" from the nearby sugar maple grove. They were soft and at times almost inaudible, but their presence suggested there was still one adult, for some reason, staying at the empty nest site most of each day. I explored in the grove and soon found the young by their faint "chip, chip" contact calls. It was the only way I could distinguish them from the adults, as they all flitted about in the leafy tree crowns.

By the following day, I again scoured the maple grove and after a long search again heard an occasional "chip" contact call and then found the group. They were now more dispersed than before, up to at least thirty yards apart, and in the dense foliage were likely out of sight of each other. The young were apparently becoming independent, now only five days out of the nest, and the male likely stayed behind to guard the nest site. Was it for them to maintain the territory to raise another clutch? If so, it would be unusual; the phoebe pair had never had a second nesting in the same year here before.

In the first days after the phoebe family had left, one of the pair had indeed several times flown directly onto the nest and stayed there for minutes at a time. But by June 24, there were no more such nest visits, and there was silence. I could no longer locate any of the family, nor hear a peep, although I searched for them several times in the following days.

Summer was rushing on. The ravens had started nesting in late February and early March, so their young were now out of the nest in May. They were following their parents, learning from them to forage. Blue jays had just now fledged. And they, too, were following their parents and being fed by them, though they were not as long dependent as the ravens. Tree swallows and chicka-dees were now fledging, and the first signs of fall approached: The fireweed was blooming, and goldenrod would quickly follow. The birds' nesting time to get the young ready for migration can be on a tight schedule, especially if, as in the case of the phoebes, there are delaying snowstorms; this year, the start of the phoebe nest building was delayed until April 29. No wonder, I thought, that many of the small birds raise only one clutch in this Northern Forest and at this elevation.

Only the female reportedly builds the nest, and it normally takes her four to fourteen days, but that is *if* she has an appropri-ate site known in advance to go to. That's no problem for those birds that can use any twig on any tree or patch of ground, but phoebes use a special site, one representing a cliff overhang, unlike any other bird now living in the Northern Forest. The site on my cabin is rare; it has the advantage of potentially saving almost two weeks of time.

And so, as I was finishing writing up my observations of this year's phoebe nesting, not having seen a phoebe or heard one for a couple of days, right after my morning coffee I went into the cabin, opened the window, and . . . a bird flushed out of the nest! My hunch was correct; the pair had cooperated as though having it planned. Silently I reached up into the nest and felt three eggs! She had just been in the process of laying an egg. Her second clutch had started, and it seemed as though it might have been foreseen as I compared observations from previous years, especially those concerning hygiene at or near the nest.

This second clutch in the same nest can be an opportunity, but it can also have a cost. Having watched phoebes over the years, I've been impressed by the enormous amounts of fecal waste a family of a half dozen young produces and drops to the ground. Ground nesters, such as the hermit thrush or ovenbird, do not *ever*, to my experience, leave a single dropping. The parents remove all. With their first clutch, these phoebes had left, compared with what they usually left, very little. But any bird completing its entire growth from hatchling to adult necessarily produces a lot of feces, and a whole clutch of them, a pile. *This* time the near absence of poop at the phoebe nest was a surprise and appeared to be deliberate.

Here in Maine, in my annual post-nesting poop count, the pair had typically left fifty to a hundred droppings under their nest by the time their young had fledged. In contrast, and to my amazement, in Vermont the parents clean up most of their young's dung as it is produced. The tree swallows, however, don't haul off any of their youngsters' poop (which piles up a considerable amount from their four or five offspring, and piling up *inside* the supposedly safe nest box). In contrast, ground-nesting songbirds such as veery or ovenbird leave not a single drop of poop near their nest, as the parents meticulously remove every single poop droplet from the young, which poop as they are fed. The "no droplet left behind" policy is an obvious antipredator strategy because poop stinks and predators learn to associate it with very fresh meat nearby. Those nests that left a poop for a predator to smell may no longer be in the gene pool. Cleanliness is or can be a matter of life and death.

My Maine phoebes had first fledged on June 16 and sparked my hypothesis that they might *this* year renest (unlike all the other years before) and try to raise a second clutch of young. But if so, they had *plans* to reuse their same nest.

On June 27, the nest that had fledged the young now held four new eggs. A very unusual event. Had our summer lengthened? Had the birds known? These two unusual behaviors—starting a second brood in the same nest and leaving less poop from the *first* brood—suggest that they had anticipated raising a second clutch in the same nest, even before the first clutch of young had left. I calculated that the pair can, by annually reusing the nest, save ten days (a ready-made nest means not needing to build another), and raising two broods in that nest saves twenty days' effort. This is a huge difference in the seasonal time constraints of rearing young in the short-summered Northern Forest. Of course, the birds would not count the days, but they certainly *feel* the seasons.

As I expected, the phoebes did almost nothing to alter the nest for the second use. It had been kept intact, and more importantly, kept unusually clean over a prolonged period of time. Given the brief Northern Forest summer season and the uncertainties of finding a suitable nest site, it may seem excessive to cut it so close, but every bit helps, and being able to use the same nest twice, provided it is in a perfect location, makes it worth picking up the poop.

I could understand that in all the hardiest of ground-nesting birds I had never once found a single smudge of poop, as strong selection pressure would have eliminated the lethal behavior of leaving it. But to now see it *optional* in the phoebe, as a matter of choice, invoked in me awe and wonder. If a phoebe can *plan*, then we are not alone. There is more to life than we can see or assume.

Five

Spreading the Chestnut Tree

In my forest, where the chestnuts now grow, the turkeys have also returned. Both are multiplying. The forest is largely a mixture of American ash, yellow and white birches, red and sugar maples, American beeches, black cherries, and some white pines, red spruces, and balsam firs. By planting the chestnuts, I breached an artificial boundary. Species are being readmitted to their ancestral home where they were part of a complex ecosystem. By planting four trees, I am helping the jays, and more, make it whole again.

THE HOMING INSTINCT, 2014

THE FOREST, LIKE ANY ECOSYSTEM, IS NOTHING *BUT* and everything *of*. An incredible number of distinct but also similar species have achieved an equilibrium of give and take for their mutual benefit. We are aware of animal cooperation in behavior, and it is our hallmark as humans, but coordination for survival *between species* is also an ancient physiological and ecological legacy. Vertebrate animals are a conglomerate of ancient bacteria that evolved to become the energy-yielding mitochondria of muscle. Other bacteria found a niche in our intestines, serving there in digestion, as do fungi-made lichens and as algae do in plants, becoming chloroplasts as energy catchers from the sun.

Symbiosis reaches far beyond cells. It extends to the relatively recent sexual reproduction by plants where the pollen became spread by animals rather than just water or wind (about 300 million years ago). It is a "recent" innovation of Earth's life, which started after billions of years of prior evolution by ferns, mosses, and horsetails. This innovation of animal-plant cooperation for pollination spread and diversified about 125 million years ago with insects, which led to other animals increasingly becoming a substitute for wind pollination. Pollination by animals reaches its most diverse and amazing degree in the tropics, with its proliferation of flowering plants, the angiosperms.

The geologically gymnosperm (conifer) spores were borne by wind (and perhaps water) and are still to the present day. But once insects evolved to use pollen as food, they began transferring the pollen from plant to plant, starting the plants' flower evolution, where primarily the insects' attraction to and manipulation of flowers ushered in the insects' preferences and behavior. Color, scent, and food rewards became significant in plant reproduction and were guided by animal behavior. Animal foraging behaviors became selective agents for the evolving symbiotic plant-animal associations, leading to the evolution of flower variety and complexity, with no end in sight in shape, color, scent, and food or other reward.

Perhaps one of the most visually conspicuous flowers is arguably the orchid *Angraecum sesquipedale* from Madagascar. It puzzled Charles Darwin in 1867 because its nectar was presented at the bottom of an over-eight-inch-length spur where seemingly nothing could reach it—until in 1903 a sphinx moth (then named *Xanthopan morganii praedicta*) was found with a long proboscis (insect equivalent of a tongue) that when unfurled reached eight inches (about five times the moth's body length), which was long enough to reach the nectar. With other animals unable to reach the nectar, the reward should generally remain great enough for such long-tongued moths to search for it in a tropical forest containing a mix of plants that are widely dispersed.

There are no such sphinx moths in the North Woods. They have likely not evolved here because the far fewer tree species grow at short enough distances between trees of the same species that wind suffices for their pollination. Instead, some, like the big poplar sphinx moth (*Pachysphinx modesta*), have a rudimentary proboscis and no longer require any food as adults. Like many others, they rely on leaves eaten in the caterpillar stage the previous summer and stored as fat through the winter by the pupa for the emerging adult.

In contrast, in the spring in Northern Forest bogs, relatively large rewards are available to bumblebees, from the first willows offering easy-to-access nectar and pollen, which is available in separate male and female flowers on respective male and female trees. After that bloom, the bees visit a variety of the plant species blooming together, one after another. Their flowers (with both sexes in the same flowers on the same plants) are sufficiently different from each species that individual bees hone their major skills to specialize on one species and minor on another that is similar. At first species bloom at once, and then single species bloom sequentially, one following another, and the bees switch "majors" (their primary species) as opposed to their "minor" (a fallback).

For many years I marked individual bumblebees with numbered tags and followed them to try to get a glimpse at what was going on, using the data to find parallels between their management of energy resources and the economic theories of Adam Smith. But my most recent close look at the sexual pollination process in the North Woods occurred inadvertently decades after I had planted several native American chestnut (*Castanea dentata*) seedlings.

I have planted trees wherever I have lived, such as an alley of various species from our woods at the family farm in Maine, or nursery apples on our (mandatory) lawn at our house in midtown Walnut Creek in California. When, in 1980, I returned to the North Woods of Maine, I happened to look in a catalog with the idea of perhaps planting a pear (or something) in my clearing in the woods that had once been the old farmhouse and barn site. My eye caught an offer for wild American chestnut seedlings for sale from a relict population thought to be resistant to the blight *Cryphonectria parasitica*, a parasitic fungus that had a century ago wiped the American chestnut off the North American continent. On a hunch I ordered fifteen seedlings and planted them next to the log cabin that I was then building along the edge of the clearing. I didn't expect much of anything but nevertheless may have had at least a whiff of a thought of potential, because I still have my receipt for the purchase. That receipt is now a treasure, saved on a dream. All the common commercial varieties of fruit trees I'd also planted are long dead, but the then almost extinct chestnuts are now in their forty-third year, thriving far beyond expectation and in their now third generation, with the forest sprinkled with at last count 1,300 offspring, spread up to at least a half mile in several directions.

There had likely never before been any of these chestnut trees here in the North Woods, at least not since the last glaciation, and so they would not have coevolved here with the native flora. Given the chestnuts' catkin-like flowers, where, unlike in willows', each has a large male top and a small female part at the base, this tree species is most likely adapted for both wind and insect pollination. So I was not surprised when these trees first began to flower after two decades and were visited by numerous potential pollinators, including various species of flies, bees, beetles, moths, and occasionally a butterfly. Fruits were produced, but most did not then contain the typical three nuts each. Soon after, when several of the trees flowered annually, most of the fruit contained the typical three fertile nuts that annually produce viable offspring. Unlike all the other forest trees, mature chestnuts flower late in August, their whole tops lit up in white above the trees' dark green foliage below, and the flowers are visible from a great distance and likely located by scent as well.

By contrast, most wind-pollinated trees bloom early in the spring *before* most insects are active and before the leaf buds open. These include ash and poplar, which, like willow, have separate male and female flowers on separate trees. Others, including alders, hazelnuts, birches, and maples, generally have both sexes on the same tree but on separate flowers.

Wind-pollinated trees predominate in the Northern Forest, where tree species are few, and with trees of the same species close to each other, wind pollination suffices. But one would expect other selective pressures in a tropical rainforest, such as the great Amazon forest in Peru, where in the Panguana research station, which is about four miles square, such issues of diversity have been studied for a lifetime by Dr. Juliane Koepcke. The Panguana reserve contains over five hundred tree species, and every tree of one species is likely distant from the next of the same species. An animal rather than the wind may thus be more able to "find" and pollinate it. For that there are many possibilities, as the forest is inhabited by fifteen thousand species of moths, fifty-two species of bats, and almost four hundred species of birds. But as in the Northern Forest, their long-term "immediate" survival is now dependent on more than pollination.

Trees are recognized as the lungs of the earth. They are important ecologically far beyond maintaining specific bee, bird, or mammal populations. And that includes us humans in addition to hundreds of thousands of other species. An estimated 17 percent of the Amazon forest has been removed for agriculture and is no longer available to capture the carbon dioxide (CO_2) out of the air, which then remains and causes global warming. This leads to more forest death, as temperatures in the tropics are rising, predicting its eventual replacement by savanna. The rate of increase of carbon dioxide is even more than it was forty-seven years ago, when in a physiology class on respiration I was shocked to learn that of the atmospheric concentrations of the various gases, carbon dioxide was for some reason increasing. These associations between species extend most prominently to ecosystems that ultimately "make" the biosphere on the planetary scale.

As the years pass, I note the transition of the forestland where I live, the changes from recent memory and the projections into the future. I am aware of the long term but increasingly attuned to the short term. The short term is the only one we see, given our brief lifetimes. That is the only relevant one in practice and there is enough there to engage us. It is not urgent to *us* and our immediate critical lists. It is not my topic of expertise, for it is out of my influence. I "see" it like I see the past, looking back, only potentially accelerating but still out of our hands. Yet sometimes I am afraid that "it" is too fast, and I worry, thinking what in the hell is going on? I worry if those changes are "natural" or caused by our inadvertent, inconsiderate, or unknown effects. Even the phoebes seemed to acknowledge at least a future. If all animals

adjust to the seasons of the year, why not those concerning coming generations?

OVER MANY SPRINGS in Maine, living at the same spot, I have
had an impression that even more was changing than I could see.
I was wondering about something I could feel in my own forest:
What has happened to the blackfly hordes in spring, and where
have the cluster flies gone that in fall blackened the windowpanes
in my cabin? Where were the crowds of bumblebees that gathered
on the meadowsweet bloom in late summer, along with the goldenrod bloom in the fall? Why worldwide are car windshields no
longer splattered with insect remnants after a long summer ride?
Is there something unseen in the air? What happens to the plastic
wrapping of every few bites of food the millions of us buy, then
eat? How long does it take for the fumes from an industrial process in the West to reach the East? It must go somewhere, and it
definitely is not into outer space.

Changes had always seemed natural to me. I suspect they still
are. But there is evermore that I do not know and can't yet par-
cel out the causes. I was, in previous years, astounded to see no
blooming of the beech trees and hence no beechnuts, and sometimes the sugar maple trees have zero flowers as well. I attribute
natural causes and find possible adaptive scenarios to explain
them. But counting the growth rings in the conifer logs in my
cabin I saw that every one of the conifers I had used (and I had
taken them randomly) had stopped growing near the *same time*
about fifty years ago. That was too abrupt to be from anything
we knew of, except forest succession—the natural process of species changing over time, usually in response to something, which

in this case is that the Northern Forest *is* here receding, and the broad-leaved trees *can* fill in, if the land is left to *be.*

On December 18, 2023, we experienced the most severe weather disturbance I had seen to date. On that night, when one might have expected a snowstorm to add to the already existing snow cover, the rain on my roof was deafening. Floods tore the tarred pavement off the local highway, and fierce winds smashed down huge trees in all directions, some right next to me and over my path to the cabin and my truck. I took the opportunity to find out which trees were the most vulnerable—it was by far the conifers, thirty-three to two in my count of the wind-felled live trees. Any look in the woods shows the same skew in mortality; conifers are by far the lowest survivors compared with broad-leaved trees. I believe "it" is simple adaptation to environment. It's more difficult for conifers now in the changing forest.

The present forest succession from the typically Northern Forest conifers to the more southerly deciduous trees represents adaptation in their reproduction as well. There had been an extraordinary crop this year of all three of the native wild cherries, the red, the black, and the choke, but I could not find one winterberry (*Ilex verticillata*) on the usually fecund shrubs that always seemed prominent all winter, keeping the robins and the bluebirds north. These birds are now gone in late August, long before winter has begun. Instead, the beautiful evening grosbeaks were here in crowds, with an unheard of sixty-five of them in a single group at my bird feeder of black sunflower seeds. I remembered them from another winter as a child when they were feeding on the seeds of white ash (*Fraxinus americana*), and I then planted a seedling of it from out of our woods alongside others near our driveway at the farm. Now, many decades later, the ash were again loaded with seeds in the fall after a spring when they had all bloomed. And there is potentially another recent precedent, or I'd like to think that it might be my aforementioned American chestnut.

TWO OF MY original seedlings have reached the forest canopy, and the largest crowns soar to sixty-five feet high. Other "seedlings" are by now catching up to the parents and producing "grand trees." One of several offspring I have transplanted along the upper portion of my driveway, where they have ample exposure to sunlight, has reached a circumference at breast level of sixty-six inches and a height of about thirty feet. In turn, one of its offspring is now the size of its grandparent. I have for over a decade been spreading the chestnut tree to friends and neighbors in New England, but several have taken root all the way to Chicago. Here in Maine, though, is their center, so far. Their thriving here now, where they had been absent recently despite the passenger pigeons who would have been spreading them, is another sign of climate change.

Growth into trees from the (recently) blue jay- and squirrel-spread chestnut seeds is chancy, as seedlings in the undisturbed forest show up for a year or two or three, but many then, as with all seeds, succumb, browsed off by snowshoe hare and deer, or else they use up their stored nutrients if shaded and then are unable to replenish their energy requirements for further growth. They may stay alive for several years, growing only slightly or not at all, but remain ready and poised for an opening. Chestnut seedlings can "hang on" in an immediate weather anomaly not only because of the energy reserves of the nuts, a legacy of the parents, but also by keeping their leaves green long after those of the other deciduous trees have shed theirs, and they acquire at least some solar energy input in the fall. It happens almost only at this time, when these seedlings are easy to locate from a distance, because almost all other broad-leaved trees have by then shed their leaves.

Blue jays are, of course, well known as "the uphill planters" because they fly uphill. We tend to more often notice the seemingly hard, even if it is easy for them. But I'm already living (nearly) on the top of a hill. Though not acknowledged, blue jays are also excellent downhill planters. And although seldom mentioned, I believe that coyotes do better work than blue jays for spreading the chestnut trees. They keep down the hare and deer populations that would munch out any little chestnut trees, especially in fall and winter. There are numerous seedlings in the shaded fast-growing balsam fir tree stand a hundred yards from the seed bearers, which snowshoe hare and deer snip off. But forestry practices create scattered forest openings, those likely for blue jays to land in to "plant," helping chestnuts to grow and eventually produce their delicious seeds and potentially their superb lumber. I'm just not so sure about the nuts to roast over an open fire. They taste best just the way the blue jays and squirrels eat them.

Even as an experienced tree climber, I'm unable to harvest the chestnuts from a tree. The fruits (called burrs), each containing three nuts, are at the tips of the long thin branches at some fifty to sixty feet or more above the ground. They are located conveniently for easy seeing from the air to specifically be harvested and picked and spread far and wide by blue jays. The three nuts per fruit become easily available to them after the four externally spiny flanges of each burr curl out, to thus offer their three seeds/nuts each. A jay can take three of these nuts into its throat pouch and fly off to hide them and later, remembering their location, retrieve and hammer them open.

WHILE BLUE JAYS are acknowledged chestnut tree planters, the squirrel's role is more aligned as seed predation, and red squirrels (*Tamiasciurus hudsonicus*) are my partners when I want to eat chestnuts. The blue jay crowd nabs those three nuts contained in a burr, the fruity part that is spinier than a hedgehog, before they have a chance to fall. Of course, the red squirrels are onto *that* tactic, and they do their best to get ahead of the blue jays to nip them in the burr. Like this: They climb to the top of the tree and there start snipping off one burr fruit after another after the nuts are ripe but just before the burr opens. This behavior may look like waste, but it is squirrel strategy. (Only the red, though; the gray squirrels love to eat chestnuts also, but they eat them right there where they are found.) The reds are hoarders and simply to reduce traveling time they come down after they have dropped a dozen or two burrs, then haul them off to their nearby cache—one that is commonly underground. I usually wait until the squirrel has snipped off about ten or so burrs, then I rush in under the tree and quickly gather them all up. If I want more, I step back and wait as the squirrel runs back up the trunk and up into the tiptop thin branches to do it again. So far, all the trees on my property (which is under a conservation easement by the Maine Forest Society) are "wild-planted" except the seven chestnut transplants framing the passageway to my cabin.

NECTAR, POLLEN, AND seeds are the least of the *product* that chestnuts and many other trees *produce.* The one thing they would not provide to many creatures, if they could avoid it, is leaves, their mini chemical factories doubling as solar panels. If they have one enemy (and they have it galore), it is the larvae of moths and butterflies. One caterpillar can't do much damage, but if it is fed and matures, it may have generated a thousand offspring the next year, and the year after that half of *those* will each generate a thousand. It is then only a small step before the tree is necessarily bare, and dead, along with a thousand times a thousand caterpillars— unless the caterpillars can avoid such things as starvation, predation, parasites, and bacterial and viral infections. But *this* happens only sporadically, because caterpillars have evolved some amazing protection strategies, aside from spines, poisons, and mimicry. My proudest achievements (or at least the most fun) have been tracking down and *finding* some of their behavioral strategies.

It may seem counterintuitive, but one way some caterpillars protect themselves from being found and eaten, and thus being able to be harmful to trees by browsing off their leaves, is to *increase* their role as leaf eaters. I will never forget the first time I came upon this, a rather sneaky strategy that I am now attuned to and that anyone can see routinely if they know what to look for. Yes, it is perhaps easy to guess after you are on to it (and for the caterpillars, hopefully birds are *not*). Many birds, of course, use caterpillars as a primary food. But to eat the leaves, caterpillars have to start from the edges and eat out sections and holes in the leaf. Those leaf cuts are what alerts birds to find and eat *them*, especially those whose main anti-bird strategy is to hide. I've been on to it since I was a ten-year-old kid.

Birds may not *think* of it, but they easily learn it, as I did through my experiments. Indeed, it used to be the main way I found those seemingly clever camouflaged leaf eaters, but birds learn fast. When I look at the ground under my chestnut trees, and almost any other broad-leaved tree in midsummer, I usually see all sorts of fresh leaves, all half-eaten, and all with only a stump left for a petiole. When blue jays find "damaged" leaves on the tree, they start looking and find the culprit. It is, of course, all to mutual advantage. It means that the tree has more solar energy input and can put more energy into flowering and producing nuts, although this would normally be insignificant. But when there is a *possible* caterpillar outbreak, and they *do* occur, then a large tree will produce no nuts.

We notice only what we learn. Now, after having tested what chickadees and blue jays do, every summer I see that the path up to my cabin is "paved" with dozens of green leaves, something that I'd never seen before.

Six

Caterpillar Pursuits and the Promethea Moth Year

Scientific discoveries, like most surprises, come by luck, and luck comes by keeping moving and having a keen nose to detect anomalies.

WINTER WORLD, 2003

TWO OF MY FIVE REMAINING CHESTNUT TREES ARE now literal giants. Some sixty feet tall, most years they produce thousands of nuts used by jays, squirrels, mice, and me. Their offspring favor the roughly 360 acres of surrounding forest and have a huge impact on it. It is like a dream come true to have them back in the American forest when it had only recently been thought they were extinct. It seems "impossible," but then so had my thought of setting "impossible" running records. It happened and they happened because I'd dared it, and that's what made it.

The forest is changed as I've been changed and as others are or will be. I *am* changed still by the last of the apple trees that I'd in my mind "seen" the pioneers plant here two centuries ago, trees we sailed across the Atlantic Ocean on British ships. We could make those trips because of the giant American white pine trees (*Pinus strobus*), many of which had come from the east side of "my" hill, and were hauled by teams of oxen down to the Penobscot River, to have been floated to the coast, to be turned into masts for the great sailing ships. I marvel and almost weep for joy at what is possible if one does what is right. What will happen when we *all* wake up, realize that we are *each* one part of the great creation that is Life of this Planet Earth, which affects every part in the long run? The "run" that is measured not just in our own lifetimes, but in the lives intertwined into one interactive *all*. When will we wake up, open our senses to the community of this great superorganism that was created over a period of untold millions of years, of which we have seconds? We are only a tiny blip compared with the All, and we only experience it once. I'm experiencing the chestnut trees now and will continue the journey to wherever it goes.

On the second day of June 2023, as dark clouds gathered over the hill, a thunderclap shattered the silence. I'd not heard one in years, although a nearby hemlock is splintered from top to bottom, so it happens; it is not unexpected. Ben Franklin's idea of deflecting lightning strikes by attraction, by putting up a metal lightning rod, had caught on a long time ago, and every farmhouse or barn in this part of Maine used to have one. But for some reason they no longer do. And as expected, after an hour or so the occasional thunder bursts became faint, and stillness resumed.

Just as there has not been a thunderstorm in the last two years, the rain this last year was unusual. My well was filled with water to the top all winter, although it is normally dry by September. Staying at the same place I *learn* more because of the comparisons that present themselves, that would otherwise not be possible; so much would drift by. *Only by contrast to something else is anything noticed.*

Most of the trees are now fully leafed out, and the beech has already sprouted new green limb shoots over a foot long, each one laden with a row of a dozen or more full-sized leaves, with more appearing at the growing tips of the tree's rapidly lengthening twigs. The new (here) chestnut trees had been quicker than all the others in putting out leaves, and they *keep* them longer, too, some right into the first days of November, while the other deciduous trees have shed all their leaves two weeks earlier. But this year the green leaves on most of the deciduous trees had been killed by an apparently late frost that they would *not* have experienced farther south in the lands of their origin. They were soon rebounding with new buds (that "normally" grow only in fall) so that they were leafing out all over again after having lost their first leaves to the late frost.

Despite these vagaries of the weather, the deciduous trees in this forest are booming, even more than I expected. I have harvested ample maple syrup from what used to be a brush patch of fir, spruce, pine, ash, red and sugar maple, simply by favoring the maple and using the spruce and fir for building. Spruce and fir are northern trees and predominate up into the Arctic. Although they are here now mainly on the mountains, they will soon be history, except at the very peak of the mountaintops. Their fading trend suggests global warming, now leading to succession. One thing is sure: The American chestnut, once a southern tree, may be just a little quick to start leafing out, but as now shown, it can recover from a frost and then grow along with the rest of the deciduous trees, if not better. It is now, for here, a tree of the future getting a good start as other species are being pushed out.

I am surprised how the red spruces are now dying, their growth diminished year by year until it stops altogether—a changing climate phenomenon. This includes even those I'd allowed into the clearing, where they had no shortage of sunshine, where all the deciduous trees are off and running at high speed, making noticeable progression by the day.

The conifers have not yet even opened their buds, but summer won't officially start for another three weeks. Who declared summer anyway? The declarations of the trees speak clearer or at least louder than we can, or ever will, because summer was just proclaimed from the heavens, loud and clear today.

NO CHESTNUT BLIGHT has been recorded in forty years, and although two trees were attacked in the roots by another fungus, they recovered. Might they be susceptible to being eaten in their crowns by another tree enemy—caterpillars? Most caterpillars are specific in their food preferences. With no American chestnut trees in this area before and hence no fungal blight and *perhaps* also no specific caterpillars, it was possible they escaped not just the blight but leaf browsers as well. That question could be hard to answer, as there was scant chance for me to assay all the leaves in the tree canopy, because there was no way I could reach into the top of the thin branches of the now sixty-foot-tall parent trees. And even if I could, how would I know if they were being attacked by caterpillars before those caterpillars denuded the tree, as they do at times the oak and maple?

Outbreaks begin with the scatter of green leaves on the forest floor, always a sure sign of mid- to late summer and a new predator on a newly vulnerable tree. Those leaves on the ground are not discarded by the trees. They are, as I described, the subtle but telling sign of caterpillars in the treetops becoming large and potentially conspicuous to birds now hunting them to feed their fast-growing chicks. Each moth or butterfly generally deposits hundreds of eggs, and the larvae become the main food of most forest birds, so in defense, many caterpillars make themselves seem invisible by various strategies, including mimicking leaves or parts of foliage, aside from the behavior of severing the petiole of a leaf after finishing their meal on it.

After noticing the first caterpillar-chewed chestnut leaves on the ground under one of my trees, I looked and found sixty-seven more partially eaten leaves on the ground. Given that many moth species are specific in their feeding preferences, I wondered: Might the caterpillar be a rare now-reviving species? Would they multiply and explode into an outbreak and become a pest? How many caterpillars did it take to drop those sixty-eight leaves? I climbed a tree to near the top to hunt and find out.

This twenty-year-old tree had strong limbs within easy reach from the ground, and I examined every limb up and into the seven-yard-high crown but to my surprise found neither caterpillar nor partially consumed leaves. The caterpillars were either well hidden, had already left the tree to pupate, or had recently been consumed by local birds such as blue jays, chickadees, or red-eyed vireos. I found none, yet clipped-off leaves appeared by the following dawn. So, these caterpillars were nocturnal. I again climbed the tree and searched more carefully, this time noting more precisely where the dispatched leaves had landed, and to my joy found a caterpillar apparently hiding on the underside of a large leaf. This caterpillar was of moderate size and covered with thin, long, snow-white "hair," with three long black tufts sticking out at odd angles melded into the leaf; from a distance it could be mistaken for a reflection of sunlight from the smooth leaf surface. It was the larva of the moth *Acronicta americana*, named the dagger moth because its three black tufts were reminiscent of daggers stuck into its pure white pelt. This caterpillar is well known for feeding on a variety of deciduous trees, and clearly it was well provided by the new tree species in this area.

I left it on its perch and brought it, along with the twig, inside the cabin for closer observation. It consumed less than half of one leaf during the night, and on departing that leaf before daylight (as I suspected it might) chewed through the petiole to detach the remainder of the leaf from the twig. It then spent all day curled up motionless and thus less vulnerable to birds—a white button-like clump—on the underside of another, yet undamaged, leaf.

This was good evidence. But I don't trust just one caterpillar. Perhaps there was more to discover. Perhaps they don't care much and a single or even a few behaviors could be incidental. However, the next morning I found *two* partially consumed leaves under the same tree, and now having an image to search for, I found two more dagger moth caterpillars. All three had eaten less than half of their typically four- to six-inch leaves at night, starting from the tip, then crawling off the leaf and, as before, chewing through the petiole to snip the uneaten remainder before hiding. All three had then settled in on the underside of a nearby leaf, where they curled into a ball of white fluff with their black "daggers" sticking out in three directions. They stayed immobile for the rest of the night and day. It's not enough for a scientific publication but is, for me, the start of one. I was excited by these observations, but there was more: as so often happens, the seeking reveals more than the sought, because it channels into the not-even-thought-of. In this case, the real surprise was at the top of the twenty-year-old chestnut tree that I had climbed.

This tree, being in the relatively open clearing by the cabin, had spread its limbs in all directions, as chestnuts routinely do where there is direct sunlight. There had been no view through the thick foliage upward. Caterpillar clues on the ground had caused me to climb into the crown, where I saw not what I was looking for, but would not have otherwise seen, and had not imagined: twenty fully formed American chestnut *fruit*. The chestnut trees were likely reproducing!

By early fall the burrs are covered in bristles, each already holding three nuts inside. In a few weeks the husks split and the jays move in. I've never seen one perch to crack the shells. Instead, they cram several nuts at once into their throat pouches and fly off, sometimes a mile or more, to bury them under leaves or soil. They come back for many of the nuts, but not all. The misses sprout. Forgotten food becomes trees.

Both *parent* trees had produced hundreds of burrs and thousands of seeds over about twenty years, but *these* burrs that were within weeks of releasing seeds were now in the crown of *this* specific tree that I had climbed to find a caterpillar, an unanticipated discovery. That means that the two parent trees I had planted forty-one years ago would this year become grandparents. That the *offspring* of trees planted as a mere afterthought so long ago were now wild and spreading far and wide (both naturally and by my distribution to friends in New England and far beyond) was worthy of a celebration.

And now, forty-one years later at dusk I stuck some of one of their offspring's leaves into my pocket, specifically those partially eaten by caterpillars (that I'd saved to sketch), and headed out the door toward the village inn to meet friends and neighbors sure to be found there for beers.

We celebrated for hours, reviewing our pasts, presents, and perhaps seasons of future human social development for possible rational behavior. We didn't get far with this as I recall, so I reached into my pocket and produced the caterpillar-snipped fresh chestnut leaves, to ask what they thought of them. Would they notice? If so, they didn't say. So I told them my story of the caterpillars and the year's earlier experiments with chickadees who flew preferentially to trees with the paper-punched leaves after having found mealworms on such trees, and the blue jays who could select, by a peck at a photo, a leaf damaged by a palatable versus a *spiny* or hairy (nonpalatable) caterpillar, who I describe as "messy eaters" because they never snip off their partially eaten leaves. They don't need to because they don't need to hide; they can nibble into the leaves and leave lots of signs here and there, feeding in full view of any bird, because what bird would try to swallow a spiny, bristly brush?

Several years later, as I write this, I'm sitting by the window, admiring the chestnut trees now reaching up into the forest canopy. I'm unable to climb to the tip-top of the *big* trees, but they are loaded with fruit, although last year they did not even flower; there was no fruit. This year, though, they are making up for it. I've been meticulous to count every burr that has fallen onto the ground (3,778 so far, with about a hundred still up in the treetop). With each burr producing these (delicious) nuts, there are enough to go around. (This does not count those already "taken around" by a group of a dozen or so blue jays, who will regularly fly a mile to find a suitable spot for them, to bury a three-pack or so.) The long-term results can be guessed at, but to be sure, some friends and I have been using GPS devices, discovering over a thousand caches.

Like a blue jay, I've been a spreader of the chestnut tree, maybe like Johnny Appleseed was for apple trees. I'd recently received an email from a now-friend in Russia who sent me a photo of one of my trees in his yard. It is the farthest flown. But there are plenty in New England, including the self- (no blue jays) planted in the neighbors' woods. This year at the end of October, the two remaining now-Methuselahs produced a bumper crop.

In birds, bees, and us, the expected is seen easily, due to what has been called the "search image," which is, by definition, the *known*. It allows staying with the profitable and not wasting time on the less rewarding. It keeps us on track with the tried and true, but at the cost of our attention being captured. The Brothers Four singing "The Green Leaves of Summer" in the 1960s got the color right and the lyrics also. It was, as they said, good to be young and close to the earth. I'm feeling young, and it is good to be in the woods enveloped by gorgeous trees with green leaves seemingly unending in space and time. But the anomalies within a grand picture are the most interesting if the contrast is great. And nothing can compare to moths.

THE PROMETHEA MOTH (*Callosamia promethia*), like a significant percentage of other insects, is, when young, a different animal than when it turns into the adult, or "imago," stage. Both survive in the same Northern Forest. It is first a gorgeous green wormlike creature decorated with two bright red knobs at the front end, and it feeds and grows from tree leaves for a summer and harvests all the energy it will ever need in the coming fall, winter, spring, and then summer, and for each season it has no resemblance to the others.

The promethea is a member of the great silk moth family, the Saturniidae. It is represented by numerous unique species in the tropics as well as in the Northern Forest, and although most of these moths fly at night, *this* species is the only one flying in the daytime—but only the males do so. In flight the almost-black males resemble an erratic bat. I'd been used to finding hundreds of these moths' caterpillars in the summer but am more familiar with the cocoons in the winter, but only because I know what to look for. Adults were likely rarely seen by anyone in over forty years until the spring of 2021, when late one afternoon, within an hour, dozens of males, then near a hundred, zoomed outside my cabin. I was shocked until I discovered a female that had that day emerged from one of the cocoons I had collected the previous fall and winter and brought into my cabin. I then fastened a thread around her waist and tied the thread onto a low branch of the black cherry tree by a window.

Within a minute or two a male had found her and was connected to her, but then within five minutes most of the crowd was leaving; her scent "calling" had apparently stopped. By late evening, the pair had finally separated, and she was then exuding eggs, sticking over a hundred onto the leaf of the cherry twig she was on. Cherry is a suitable food for the caterpillars of this species, although white ash is locally their preference. The cocoons, however, can later be found attached on almost any tree twig.

WHEN MY FEMALE slipped out of her cocoon, she would not have taken a bite of food since the previous summer. She stopped any and all intake for the rest of her and her eventual new form— the moth—from a day or two before she had spun her cocoon. She could not, because that cocoon encased her for the next eight or nine months.

That cocoon, with her in it, had then dangled from a tree branch all fall, winter, and spring, fully camouflaged by the then long dead leaf that the caterpillar had wrapped around herself. It had become part of her cocoon, shutting off all contact with the outside for the next ten months. Neither would she nor any of the flying males feed now, as adults.

The caterpillar's last food would have been a green leaf, which it chewed and then digested the previous summer. Leaves contain few calories, and flight is a hugely energy-demanding activity; thus, all of these *flying* moths would within a couple of days have exhausted their remaining meager energy stores and be rendered barely able to move before dying. However, they had survived the months of the Northern Forest's subzero temperature, and all winter long their pupae would have been nutritious helpless nutrient-filled nuggets for the many hungry predators. Each is, however, designed so that only very rarely would a bird, squirrel, mouse, or shrew either find one of these such camouflaged cocoons or, if so, be able to reach inside the silk cocoon it is wrapped in. The cocoons can be seen, but they are nearly invisible, as they mimic a stray bit of dried leaf remaining on a twig, due to the caterpillars' behavior in constructing it.

Different caterpillar species have their own antipredation features. The promethea caterpillar's cocoon is constructed so that the caterpillar is wrapped in a large leaf, and the thread from the cocoon is a continuous thread wrapping the cocoon to the leaf petiole, and from there solidly attaching the petiole to the twig, thus holding the soon dead leaf so it cannot be shed and at the same time leaving a sock-like exit from the twig end. For contrast, the thick and solid cecropia moth caterpillar *also* attaches a loose bag-like cocoon onto a twig, but then spins a *second* cocoon layer inside it. So even if a predator managed to successfully penetrate the first cocoon shell, it would find no pupa. It would likely be fooled because the pupa is inside a *second* even harder shell. No exit hole is left in *this* cocoon, but the moth of this species, when it emerges, secretes a saliva that dissolves the cocoon silk to create an exit hole.

The promethea moth pupa, despite being camouflaged, can be seen by us from a ten-yard distance. But what we "see" is a curled leaf, and many trees retain some of their leaves curled like that into winter, providing a perfect cover. However, although the trick is that the cocoon is made using the real leaf as camou- flage, by wrapping it tightly about the caterpillar, it is so tight that the caterpillar can't turn around in it, so while constructing the cocoon, the caterpillar *must* leave a sock-like exit hole at one end for the eventual moth's exit about nine or ten months later. The space in the cocoon is so tight that when finished making it, the caterpillar *must* be facing that exit hole or the moth would be trapped inside and of course die. They "never" do. I have opened hundreds of cocoons (to check for wasp parasites) and have never found a pupa whose head end was facing the wrong way.

A caterpillar can turn around and face another direction. A pupa cannot, and so, prior to settling in after the silk cocoon construction (and waiting to shed its skin and become the hard pupa), the flexible caterpillar can move back and forth, from one end to the other, depositing silk thread at both ends. However, when it stops to eventually shed its skin and become the pupa, it can no longer turn around; it *must* face the eventual exit that the eventual adult moth would use, nearly a year later in the hanging leaf. That entrance is then in the "up" direction, and that leaf will not fall off the tree, because at the entrance the caterpillar had expended silk all over the leaf petiole and wrapped that silk thread around the twig precisely where the petiole is attached. In this way, no animal can grab the cocoon and fly off with it, as a blue jay might, trying to hold the cocoon by its feet up against a solid branch to hammer into it. But now I wondered, how does the caterpillar know to face in the right direction ten months before it would need to exit as an adult?

The simplest hypothesis is that the caterpillar uses the "*up*" side for the exit sleeve of the eventual moth. However, the simplest and the seemingly obvious is not necessarily right, as shown in tests. When the caterpillars were ready to start spinning their cocoons, I put them into a cage with leaves that were *detached* from their twigs, lying *horizontal* on the cage floor, so no up-down orientation was possible. With this forced option, what would the caterpillars do?

I watched to find out. After finishing their feeding stage, they hesitated, and then searched as if disoriented, but eventually they still used these detached leaves to roll themselves up in and to then spin their cocoons shaped inside as usual. If orienting is simply by direction as such, then half of them should have ended up facing the wrong direction. To my surprise, however, they all *still* faced the entrance they had left when they had encased themselves in the tough silk prisonlike shell. These results cannot, for obvious reasons, be based on logic, for no caterpillar can know what it turns into or why it spins silk, yet every step of the process shows the correct precision in a trajectory adding one change after another. It is behavior inscribed by the process of natural selection, first proposed by Charles Darwin in 1859, that applies to structure as well as behavior and extends to the ecology of ecosystems, depicted in Darwin's analogy of "the tangled bank" of a tropical forest. It applies to the North Woods as well and came to mind at a favorite real bank at the end of the path I routinely traveled to a brook, as I collected most of my promethea cocoons and later caterpillars along the way.

ALDER STREAM IS a brook a half mile down through the woods from camp. Photos of a hundred years ago show kids swimming there, and there was then a "camp" there, because when you look into the bushes there you find the frame of a vehicle, possibly a "camper" on wheels, along with other remains, such as bedsprings and possibly a refrigerator. In other words, it is a trash heap, but you have to look hard to see it now.

I reached the pool by a path I have cleared through the woods, and I jogged down to continue the tradition of swimming where the beavers were first. The remains of their lodge are still there at the edge of it, but it is overgrown with brush, and I know what it was only because I saw it around five decades ago when it was still possible to decipher, when beavers were still being trapped farther downstream. I wasn't happy about trapping them right on my premises, but I'm sure they will return, just as the wildness of the place is back.

I would not have found the beaver lodge remnant then except for a winter wren that was singing there in the dense brush. I wanted to find its nest. I'd often been down to the brook with my friend Bobo, the great horned owl. My several (by then long since fledged) crows came eagerly along, too, after they and the owl had settled their relationship by being able to anticipate what to expect from each other. It was near the end of my experimental study of whether crows hate owls instinctively or if they learn from the experience of others. (It was the latter.) Bobo, who had the habit of following me whenever I headed into the woods with my .22 rifle, had likely anticipated a fresh meal of red squirrel on our way there.

NOW, FORTY YEARS later, I missed my companions (a lot), but I had another agenda, one not so grand: swimming. This is the only place in the brook with enough depth and length for a reasonable swim, and at the age of eighty, I wanted to find out if I could improve athletically. I had at one time mastered the butterfly stroke, being able to do fifteen of those athletic strokes in a row. I jogged down to the pool every day to do a few, if not more if I could, being pleased that at the end of the summer I got to forty strokes—two times back and forth the whole length of it. It didn't diminish my running, either, but the main gains were, as is usual, ancillary.

I'd not been the only one using that pool. One day it contained a merganser, a bird that would be at home far away in the ocean in salt water. But sometimes they wander and get lost and in unfamiliar surroundings screw up. Once one landed on the local tar road of Route 156. It then could not lift off without a little help. This one also: The length of the pool was too short, with rapids at both ends. I jumped into the pool with it, where it could apparently not see what was above the water surface, and it swam back and forth by me until I grabbed it on a swim-by and tossed it into the air as high as I could, which was high enough for it to leave without a crash into the forest.

Visitors to the pool notwithstanding, I got acquainted with the locals, mostly a huge shoal of minnows, and we soon had fun. Every time I was naked, ready to dive in, I'd catch a few grasshoppers in the grass on one side of the pool. I'd throw one after another of the grasshoppers into the water, and they stayed afloat, but their swimming technique was poor—they just kicked with their hind legs—and the movement alerted the minnows, who always scrambled among the twenty or thirty or so for who would get the hopper. After a few weeks, these fish were so eager and undiscerning that they came up to grab even dead ones, and then even any bits of floating debris, provided I'd tossed it in.

Meanwhile, a large green frog that perched along the shore's edge got in on the game. It was now minnows versus frog in the catch-the-hopper game. The frog was much shier than the minnows, but after a few weeks it got to know me and sometimes came out of its lair at the pool's edge, even before I tossed the grasshoppers into the mix.

There was only one surprise: I didn't see a single brook trout, although this is a well-known "trout stream." The fish had to be there, and I suspect they favor the more shaded areas, perhaps where there is water roiled up or over rocks. I'll have to try sometime, but I haven't fished for trout since I was a teenager, with my mentor Phil Potter, who took me fishing up country, where the brooks run fast, deep, and hard and fishing was a team sport. Like so much, it takes at least two, where the snagging of a trout, the wonder of a caterpillar, or the joy from a crop of chestnuts is shared and passed on. Humans are for sure social mammals. Goodness expands upon passing and lives on, I think, forever.

Part III

Interbeing

Seven

Birds, Bees, Beetles, and the Shiest Animal in the Woods

Ironic as it may seem, as intensity of competition increases, one of the standard evolutionary solutions to it is more cooperation.

ONE WILD BIRD AT A TIME, 2016

B Y THE END OF JULY, WHEN THE WOOD FROGLETS are leaving their natal pools, many birds have nested, and since, unlike wood frogs, they are limited to mostly a half dozen or so eggs per clutch, some are on their second clutch. Aside from a male goldfinch, my bird feeder seems abandoned, full of black sunflower seeds. The woods are silent except for a red-eyed vireo and a hermit thrush, each at their respective territory—the maple grove and the sugar maples. But strangest of all is a sudden near absence of blue jays. I didn't pay attention in past years, just taking spring, summer, fall, and winter for granted as they sped along. To what had the birds responded?

There are no obvious changes that I can see, except that the steady rains of June have stopped, and there is now sunshine. Otherwise, the trees have now leafed out. The main thing I can think of that would have changed for birds is that parental obligations have now passed, like the pool suddenly empty of wood frogs: The early loud courting and the then nest building and frantic rearing of young are done. But then I'd expect to see the woods now swarming with young birds due to multiplication. Are they merely hidden in the dense foliage extending in all directions? Have the constant rains been disastrous to them? Are they not seen because they have been so well fed they have become sedentary? That's a possibility, but I should at least hear the vireo in the distance, the crow a half mile away, or the otherwise always present blue jays.

I see few insects as well—not even a single horsefly, and only rarely a dragonfly. Blackflies were present earlier, but compared with the swarms I'd experienced in the past, they are absent this year.

Surrounding the cabin are walls of green, and in the last hour of absolute stillness I have seen two warblers and a robin. No leaf has twitched or jiggled. One small moth flew by. Have the birds left to metaphoric greener pastures? If so, how? A couple of weeks ago a blue jay was hopping around in the chestnut trees then in flower and I wondered why this bird, the main planter of the seeds of this tree and also oaks and beech in this and most Northern Forests, was seemingly paying attention to this tree. Flowers bring fruit, although that would normally not be for another two months, and as it turned out, this was the first time these trees had no fruits or nuts at all.

Could the jays come back anticipating the crop ahead? We might automatically dismiss such logic, but if we do, we may miss a discovery, and it is my passion and pleasure to see something new and to recognize it, too. That is what being alert and taking note and writing things down is all about. Behaviors are not only learned, but also inherited, triggered by specific stimuli. Birds migrate in the fall to specific locations thousands of miles south, many without "knowing," as they'd never been there before. I'm anxious now and look forward to the fall nut season already, although, as it turns out, the oaks and the beech haven't produced any fruits or nuts either.

The jays had, since early spring, fed daily next to my window, first on the sunflower seeds I provided, then also on the small red cherries of the wild pin cherry trees. The black cherries had bloomed earlier, but none of them now have a single fruit remaining. The choke cherries are not yet ripe, but they are, like the apple trees, so thickly loaded with fruit this year that the limbs are dragging down branches, some even breaking. The beeches have not bloomed for many years.

Last year the winterberry bushes fruited after a year of no fruit far and wide in the forest. Likewise, last year the red oak had a bumper crop, but this year are barren. Last year the sugar maples didn't show a flower; this year they bloomed profusely. The American ash bloomed profusely, too, and then their seed produced what was noticed by many as "the year of the evening grosbeak invasion" in northern New England. Almost every sugar maple tree above a certain size was and still is loaded with samaras to be shed into the wind in another month, to then twirl like propellers, gaining some distance from the shade of their mother trees, on the very remote chance of becoming a tree.

Fruits are the "legs" of the tree, distributing their seedlings to where they may or may not be able to become rooted for life. There are advantages to the trees for timing the various blooms and then seeds that support first insects and then birds and mammals, in an orchestra of events and interactions. The specific times of blooming, fruiting, and seed setting have potential adaptive consequences as they affect the lives of both the pollinators and the seed dispersers. The deciduous forest trees that disperse seeds by animals require edible fruit, which would have the most potential impact (because of size and abundance) on the animals of the forest if offered when there is no competition from other food sources. However, their longevity allows them time and opportunity to wait—perhaps years—and permits long intervals without producing any seed to then potentially seed at the same time locally, a behavior that may be considered a "strategy" that prevents their seed predators from reaching such high population densities that all their seeds get eaten rather than planted.

Pollination for sexual reproduction may require attracting pollinators that are willing to fly far, especially in the tropics, where the long-distance pollinators consist of hummingbirds, bats, and sphinx moths. The flowers are then baited with lots of nectar in their stamens. In the Northern Forest, with the same species growing close together, less nectar as bait is required, until sometimes none, where the flowers have pollen in large amounts spread by spring winds, preferably before the blooms are shielded by leaves. Seeing the trees' adaptations reveals the forest in beauty beyond the visual, but only through the lenses of time. In consuming these nascent potentially new baby trees, the pollinators and seed dispersers are "predators" as well. This, to us, nearly invisible dance of bee and bird pollinators, bird and mammal seed dispersers, and predators is contrasted by the work of beetles that dispatch whole trees.

BEETLES PLAY A central role in the Northern Forest. Although most stay hidden from our eyes, they are conspicuous in what they do. Every tree ends up, after if not long before death, riddled under its bark with dense networks of the trackways of beetle larvae. Trees that weaken and can no longer defend themselves soon attract beetle hordes that deposit eggs. In summer, as I chopped into a spruce tree to make a log, attracted by its plumes of the scent, long-horned beetles flew in to deposit their eggs. The larvae are often generally safe, as they grow over a year or more in their long tunnels chewed into and throughout the wood, and fungi then enter and start decay. The trees' remains, including fallen leaves and cast branches feeding fungi of many sorts, become enveloped in layers of lichens and moss, under which other beetles, wasps, and moth pupae hibernate through winter.

We see and appreciate only what we know, and I got to know plenty of beetles when I was a kid. Beetles were my first love, long before even bees. It was back in the Hahnheide forest, while we were eating crows and mice when we could get some as we arrived as refugees in Germany after our flight from Poland with nothing. Needing to catch mice was not a privation. For me it was a gift, because it led to beetles, which are so many (about 350,000 species described so far), so diverse, and perhaps so beautiful that famed twentieth-century British evolutionary biologist and geneticist J. B. S. Haldane declared that if God had created all living organisms on Earth, then he must have had "an inordinate fondness of beetles."

At age five or six, I had a special fondness of the "Laufkäfer," literally "running beetles" (family Carabidae), which are incredibly beautiful. These beetles, however, are no threat to trees. They are ground-hugging carnivores of other insects, which fell into the pit traps my father dug in the German forest to catch shrews and mice.

Aside from hunting his ichneumon wasps, Papa's byline was digging up tree stumps (occupying troops had taken many trees) to sell as firewood in Trittau, the neighboring town. After he got a stump excavated, there would be a hole in the ground, and he smoothed its sides to make it a pit trap to catch the mice and shrews. My mother skinned them, of course, before boiling them to eat, as well as preparing specimens to hopefully sell to American museums. Even though there was no postal service in 1945, Papa's Dutch friend Piet Hart Nibbrig could later send them to America via Holland. Most beetles that fell into a pit trap would eventually find a way to escape, so Papa put moss on the pit bottoms that drop-ins could hide under.

These northern German forest carabid beetles had only Latin names, and I learned them from one of two little books on beetles that the Hahnheide forester, Rolf Grutzmann, gave me. Much later, Papa took me to the museum in Kiel, where I got to see the beetles pinned in the collections there, and as the curator opened the boxes to show them to me, I recognized and whispered their Latin names. With that book I graduated to other beetle families, including those that bury mouse carcasses as food for their larvae.

Beetles are the great recyclers. I have watched them consume almost anything, from huge elephant dung balls, each turning into hundreds of beetles, to tree leaves, the pollen in flowers, and dying or dead trees for similar resurrections. Beetles also consume the remains of dead animals after dogs, cats, ravens, fly larvae, and all else has taken their turn. Burying beetles are to mice what dung beetles are to animal dung. Their carcass disposal activity is arguably an "eco-service" of the forest. The numerous but seldom seen burying beetles (genus *Nicrophorus*, aptly named after the Greek word *nekrophorus*, meaning "burying the dead"), take over where the ravens left off in the spring. The beetles' work is strictly summertime work, the season when the soil is moist and soft for burrowing; it is also the time when fly larvae, maggots, compete for the same resource by simply inserting their eggs directly onto the various crevices and fur of the carcasses and then potentially, by their great numbers, consuming a mouse or bird carcass in several days.

The bodies of the mice and small birds that the beetles bury are in size to them like a mature African elephant would be to one of us, but these beetles have no shovels or other tools to aid them in their work. Yet, they manage to bury mouse carcasses of that proportional size in sometimes an hour or less.

When one beetle discovers a carcass that can't be buried where found, it makes excursions in all directions until it finds soft soil. It then moves the carcass and buries it there. I have seen one recruit another, presumably a potential mate, as if right out of the air. The process is simple—it stands still, with its rear end up into the air, and exposes a gland from which it then emits, I presume, a sex scent. I can't claim to know how the eventual pair come to an agreement about where to carry the carcass, but I have seen how they do it. To find out I lay on my back under a screen with a mouse carcass on it to observe the technique of carcass transport.

Their method requires them to be upside down on the substrate surface of whatever the carcass happens to be on. There, instead of walking on it, they stay fixed in place and walk with feet up but on the carcass above them, facing in the chosen direction. After walking the carcass one body length, they turn around and do it anew, until the carcass is hitched along to reach the soft burial ground. They then burrow under it, pushing out soil to the sides so that it gradually becomes lowered into the ground. The pair will then, I presume, at some point mate, and eggs will be deposited on the carcass. The larvae will consume it and then pupate in the nearby soil. However, before the hole deepens and the carcass is out of sight, it is usually also being visited by blowflies, who would have had time enough to insert eggs. Their quickly emerging maggots would make short work and consume the mouse, otherwise to be used as food intended for the beetles' larvae, not the flies'. But for that problem the beetles have an ally, one that was long thought to be a parasite of them: mites.

Nicrophorid beetles are usually seen "crawling" with many mites, a seemingly disgusting sight, with the mites once thought to be predators. Instead, they are in symbiosis with the beetles, helping them. They are hitching a ride, using the beetles to deliver them to the small animal carcass to be buried. Once there, they jump off to feed on the fly eggs and young maggots, thus indirectly preserving the carcass as food for the beetles' larvae.

The beetles I watched (*Nicrophorus tomentosus*) are gorgeously marked with bright orange on their pitch-black wing covers (elytra)—beetles' first pair of wings that have through evolution been modified to become protective body shields. A beetle at rest has this pair of pseudo-wings folded over its back, and in any insect collection the protocol is to pin the specimen through the mid- to upper portion of the back, through the elytra and always on the right side. This is thus how I had also preserved my specimens of all sorts of beetles, including these.

However, now I was dealing with live beetles, and they showed another side. Watching one land I saw a flash of *yellow* just before it folded its elytra wings over its back and as it flew off sounding remarkably like a bumblebee.

How could a beetle change its bright orange and black markings to yellow, any more than a tiger could hide its black stripes? How could they do it instantly?

Picking up a beetle, I lifted its elytra and saw that the *underpart* was yellow! Unlike all other beetles, these were not flying with their upper original "wings." Instead, they twisted around at the moment of flight, hiding the upper orange and black surface and displaying the lower yellow surface like that of a bumblebee's often fuzzy surface. The effect was that in flight they were mimicking bumblebees!

Birds of many species routinely catch flying insects but will not grab another bumblebee after having done so once, as that would be like us hugging a bear by mistaking it for a beagle. This may seem unlikely, but the reverse once happened within walking distance of my cabin in the Maine woods.

A RABBIT HUNTER within a mile or so of my cabin "lost" his beagle; it simply didn't return to him as it had always done before. But since the dog had a radio collar, the hunter traced it, and the signal led him to a bear's den containing a female with her two cubs. The beagle was inside with the cubs, and the sow (female bear) would not allow the beagle to leave. To her, whatever was in the den was to be held and protected as though it could only be one of her cubs.

The hunter summoned the local game department for help. They sent a warden who tranquilized the sow and removed the perfectly healthy dog. One could envision a similar scenario with a person adopting a bear cub, as our bonding urge may also be strong. And indeed, I do have a photograph as proof. It is of my father in Myanmar (called Burma at the time) in bed with Dickie, a young bear he had adopted when the locals there in a mountain forest had brought it to him. Dickie loved to cuddle in bed with Papa, as I did also when I was little, to hear bedtime stories. The specific content of his stories, like scent to a bear, are vague to me now, but the truth is it matters less than the having been there.

A cub, or at least a small bear, once visited me at the cabin. I heard something rummaging through the woodshed. There had been no food there, perhaps the remains of an apple. I watched the cub as it came out and then leisurely walked off into the woods, and that's where bears belong.

The American or black bear (*Ursus americanus*) inhabits the woods around my cabin. It is seldom seen, and so the times I have seen one are well remembered. The closest I came to one, or vice versa, was about four yards from me when I chased it off. I'd been sitting where I'm sitting now as I write this and looked out the window as usual to my bird feeder filled with sunflower seeds. The feeder was hanging from the limb of the immediately adjacent white birch tree, and there was a huge bear standing on its hind legs reaching for it. Realizing that its behavior, given the rewards, could be habit-forming, I rushed out and yelled. Its response was instant—its front paws returned to the ground and that bear dashed off across the fields, down toward the woods. It was fast enough, I suspect, to have been able to outrun Usain Bolt, the Olympic gold medalist sprinter. I had no urge to pursue but did enjoy the show.

On reaching the woods, the bear stopped suddenly, stood up again, and looked back at me, in what seemed to me, a human way. It may not be surprising, as I had read somewhere that a shaved bear and a naked human body would, side by side, look much alike.

It seems to me that the black bear is the shiest animal in the woods. I had likely chased others without knowing it. But one I never saw or heard left tracks that were memorable, especially to my nephew Charlie Sewall, while we were deer hunting. We were widely separated, and the plan was for me to amble toward him real slow and easy, hopefully jumping a big buck along the way. I took my time in the silent woods and heard not a rustle despite the recently fallen leaves. It was a typical walk . . . until I reached Charlie. He had stood for an hour when he suddenly heard a loud crashing, and something ran at full speed directly from where he had been expecting either a deer or me, but it was a huge bear. The bear, propelled by fear, did not notice what was ahead. Charlie had no intention of shooting it, and the bear had no intention of stopping or taking the time to look closely where it was going, except away from me, who had spooked it. Luckily, it then saw three yards ahead and swerved around an ever-more anxious man holding a loaded rifle. The huge bear veered off at the last moment, and disaster was avoided.

We have instincts just like all animals, but most of us now live long enough to have seen more and can acknowledge what lies ahead. And by being able to look back and into the lives and minds of others, we are apt to find similarities if not commonality. These similarities are now mostly legends on cave walls, and the legend persists that Rome was founded by Romulus and Remus, who were lured into a den. Was it a wolf or a bear? To our ear now that legend sounds a bit far-fetched, but it is not impossible.

Our cave-dwelling ancestors in the ice ages of Europe inevitably lived closely with the cave bear (*Ursus spelaeus*) and held a high respect, if not worship, of it. Even now, although most of us, even those living in the North Woods, are of necessity distant from bears because they know us as their greatest if not only enemy. As was convincingly proven by "bear whisperer" Ben Kilham of New Hampshire, who has made a profession of caring for orphaned bears and many others, they can be our friends.

A Culture of Persistence

I have come to touch the world and the travails of a totally different yet kindred being that makes me feel less alone. I've also seen lots of morning stars and sunsets, felt alive in the snow and rain, sensed the cycling of pulsating life and silent death, found new human friendships, forgotten old traumas, and felt passion and peace.

MIND OF THE RAVEN, *1999*

THE NORTHERN FOREST CAN IN WINTER BE VACATED only by those of exceptional flight and orientation abilities. I just have to make the most of it, and that includes entertainment, and since I'm not watching a TV, especially since I have never owned one and never will, I'm ready to take full advantage of whatever transpires even when it is least expected, and that's most of the wildlife.

For me as a youngster that included caterpillars, beetles, snakes, mice, bats, and a baby porcupine. My mother had her chickens in the house and took walks outside with her raccoon, but the latter got killed, not by Hector, her big shaggy dog, but by the neighbors' dog. She had a monkey, too, but it got too smart for almost everyone and became unruly, and so Affe ended up in an institution: the Chicago Zoo. My father, when in Persia, acquired a panther (leopard) as well as Dickie the bear from Burma, and both ended up in the Berlin Zoo.

Aside from a baby porcupine and now and then a transitory bat, snake, turtle, hamster, squirrel, mouse, insect, or bird, I prefer my animals in the wild. The one drama that I know is real on many a long night in the Maine cabin is the coyotes' singing, perhaps the second best of a mammal that there is, a most wild and exuberant social serenade in nature that can be attended free at any time, whenever they happen to perform.

Coyotes sing in concerts, but with no apparent conductor. Individuals of at least half a dozen to a dozen chime in and out by their own spontaneous volitions. There may at first be just a slow yowl that starts things off, followed by some yips and yaps, but then all commence into a communal mélange, becoming ever livelier as more join in, and then finally, finally—as if by hitting a switch—silence. There may not be another performance for weeks or months, and after one of these events I wonder what they mean, who the intended audience is, if any, although certainly it is not for us, which to me makes it extra special.

Coyotes *are*, of course, dogs, although generally thought less worthy, even though the differences between a coyote and a wolf or German shepherd or even a poodle are so slight that they can, and sometimes do, interbreed. The dogs we have as friends and companions are descendant of those wolves that once dared to come close to our campsites, where we early humans were butchering the woolly mammoths that we killed by slow torture after we'd driven them into a bog, where they got stuck and became helpless to flint-tipped projectiles. I'd wager we didn't treat bears and the Neanderthals hibernating in caves or crude shelters much better when we got hungry and ran out of other game.

Culture can persist a long time, even in birds. All over the New England landscape, ravens were once shot on sight, and those here in most of New England still fly away from humans, even when they see them from a distance. That behavior is a cultural trait, inherited and passed on and on and on. When one raven fears a human and flies off in fright, the others seeing it learn instantly what was once and therefore likely now is fearsome. In Alaska, at an Inuit village, I was surprised to see ravens acting as calm as pigeons, just as we would have been of wolves coming to our campsites thousands of years ago, when we hunted the then-ample megafauna and left them the bones and entrails.

I THINK OF those starlings in Africa that routinely ride on the backs of the fierce Cape buffalo—the mbogo—and giraffes, picking off parasites and biting flies like the ones that almost killed a companion of mine as he stepped into the bushes at Mount Meru, in Tanzania, as he was showing me the way up the mountain. I think of the white herons following grazing megafauna through the grass, grabbing the grasshoppers that take flight, and the swallows that follow the mowing machines that flush flies. I think of the men of the Hadza group of northern Tanzania, who follow a little bird, the honeyguide, which makes twittering calls to both humans and the honey badger. Both recognize the bird's signal to be guided to a bee colony that yields honey for us, leaving the larvae and cocoons for the badger.

How did these cultures get started? They did not start or persist with the coyotes, ravens, or the bears in the Maine woods, who all have a long history of us. But could there be an exception to the learning passed down by culture? If so, it would have to be social, but only of the positive kind to whom the information spread is empathic, not malevolent culture passed on.

———

IT WASN'T EVEN autumn in Maine yet, and as usual one lone adult raccoon, just like my mother's, was sniffing around my cabin, perhaps because a hairy woodpecker had been busy scraping the still-in-shell sunflower seeds from my bird feeder, to find the rare one without a shell on it. This was in contrast to a second woodpecker who also visited the bird feeder, but took one seed at a time and flew to the nearby sugar maple tree and jammed the seed into a crack in the bark to hold it, so she could then hammer it and crack it open. The raccoon was scraping around in the woodpecker-generated seeds on the ground and taking them into its mouth so fast it must have been swallowing them whole.

I watched, softly mumbling at it as I stepped outside, making sure I was not looking at it directly so as not to make it feel targeted. I then casually sprinkled some freshly popped popcorn as though I were a food dispenser, still murmuring to it from a distance. The raccoon hesitated briefly and then dismissed me to pay more attention to the sunflower seeds. *That* was huge progress! I ventured closer, kneeled, and held out my hand to let her see me offering more popcorn. To my surprise, it ambled over and picked up some I had sprinkled onto the ground, and I made sure I walked away in the other direction.

The next day "she" showed up again, and I asked "her" (to make it more personal) to come to me, which she did. She appeared healthy, and after a couple more visits on subsequent days she was standing up on her hind legs, taking food directly out of my right hand. She used *her* hands to grasp the food out of mine to then lift it up to her mouth. Me, one-handed with my new iPhone, even managed to catch her in the act, to have proof of what would otherwise have been impossible to believe and would have likely been dismissed: a wild raccoon acting like a puppy, looking me right in the eye and taking popcorn out of my hand. This was more contact than I would have even dreamed, a trusting that instigated my reciprocation.

The raccoon became a memory for weeks, but reappeared on the evening of July 6, and with her came three or four fair-sized kits. She was nearby under the bird feeder. Her little ones twittered like baby birds, but she was not in the least agitated. I hurried inside and returned with a handful of my intended lunch—some crackers with peanut butter and two boiled eggs—in one hand and my flashlight in the other. She now unhesitatingly walked up to me and took the cracker, then reached up to try to take my flashlight, too, putting it briefly into her mouth for a taste, apparently thinking that if it was in my hand then it must be food.

That is when I knew who she was. She trusted me enough to expect me to bring only food. I did not relinquish the flashlight, left her two eggs instead, and went back inside to go to sleep. For a while I continued hearing the young ones chittering.

In a few days, they were a memory and a mystery, as none of them showed up again. I have no idea what happened to them, but something must have. I had on some nights heard gunshots in the forest, and I heard by the local gossip grapevine that someone was setting out bait in the woods to attract and "kill off the coyotes."

IN MY CONTINUING adventure in the North Woods, I returned to my mainstay companions, birds. The annual hunting season was over for me, but the raven and the raven pair that had come with Charlie and me near the cabin, had trailed us, were very much still here and once again on my mind. Their charm was derived from memory of ravens past. They had nested in tall pines almost within sight of the cabin, and I had in the last two weeks heard the couple there like clockwork at first light calling back and forth. They always left and didn't return until dusk. I put out bait as of yore. No crowds came as they had in decades earlier.

The raven is a revered bird of the North Woods and beyond. Just ask the Ravenmaster at the Tower of London. Ask the woman who told me of the raven that came to her as she was picnicking on Mount Denali, sharing her food, and not just the given, but also prying apart her fingers to get what she held. Go to the desert by a cliff and see one tumble down from the sky in aerobatics you won't believe. Go to Yellowstone and see them open the pockets of snow machines to check them out for food. And then remember, or try to, that it really is a bird and that there are thousands of species, each with something to offer when we can get close enough to them and engage in trusting contact.

Ravens are the earliest nesters in the North Woods, likely because winter is when carcasses, a main food, are to be found— also, perhaps, because as a large bird it takes them a long time to complete a nesting cycle, with the young learning from their parents and being with them long after they have fledged. Perhaps they do this because much of their behavior is learned, and it takes time, especially as they associate with the big and frequent predators in the North Woods and beyond—wolves, and humans with their dogs, the offshoots of wolves. Ravens take naturally to big game and their hunters, and we use them as guides to the caribou and other prey. In the Maine woods, I got to know ravens personally, especially one I'd hand-reared decades ago and named Goliath, who as an adult bonded to White Feather, a wild-caught adult.

While Goliath, an adoptee of mine from the nest, had experienced only affection and companionship from me, he was, nevertheless, smitten by White Feather. I had captured her when she was a fully adult female who, if she had a mate, would then have been separated from him. She now would be identified by humans by a white patch of plastic with a number on it attached to her right wing. She was then released into a gigantic (16,000-cubic-yard) chicken-wire aviary built into the woods, along with numerous other ravens, including Goliath, who was then a single adult male. He displayed and apparently liked her very much, so I gave them both their own private aviary. She eventually liked him, too, and after a year the couple nested in a crate I'd made for them and attached to thick branches on the bottom half of a thick spruce tree in their aviary. After they and all the other ravens were released back into the wild, Goliath and his then mate remained and built their nest in the shelter of the crate and raised four young to fledglings. They and their young went freely in and out at least for a while, but then abandoned it and built a nest nearby, as *their* aviary.

Something extraordinary happened one morning before daylight. Something never experienced before, nor since. It was still dark when I was awakened by an excited raven, calling from up high in the sky. I had *never* before heard a raven at what appeared to be displaying by "singing" at night. This was so unusual that I got up and went outside to witness the impressive performance. A *pair* of ravens were flying/fluttering at great height and at the same time emphasizing the display by a series of loud staccato-sounding vocalizations. I'd never heard anything like it, but since it was close to another nesting time it likely had significance for that. It was most weird, though, because my favorite couple, Goliath and White Feather, were by now well established. Yet, a third raven occasionally called from nearby in the forest, one that was apparently excluded from this sky dance. I wondered, was the sky dancer perhaps White Feather's previous mate who had now finally found his long-lost mate?

After that spring, whenever I saw the pair, a *third* raven always seemed to be straggling behind. I'd never heard of or seen a three-some raven arrangement. Who was the hanger-on? What was going on? Given that White Feather had a *black* mouth lining right from the beginning, showing she was an adult (even yearlings still have pink mouth linings), I suspected she was already a paired adult when we had captured and confined her with Goliath. If so, she had been separated, but so had he, her former mate. In turn, Goliath would have felt his mate stolen as this (to him) unknown male had shown up in Goliath's long-held territory at the most sensitive time for such connections.

After this sky dance, it was routine for me to see two ravens flying as a pair and a third tagging along. Their identity markers had long been lost, so I could not identify them, as they were associating with each other and not with me. And then, after a new nest was being built, it was soon destroyed, presumably by the former mate. Goliath had become wild by now—was no longer coming to me.

Ravens learn from each other; when one of a crowd flies off in fright from a human, then all who see it are spooked. When one feeds at an animal carcass, others are prone to join it. I think Goliath had by then, since his bonding with White Feather long ago, avoided me because White Feather, the wild raven, had inadvertently "warned" him of me, of what she must have remembered as I had captured her and clamped a white tag onto her right wing. Warning is routine—a mere gesture can suffice. She had, after all, been lured into a wire contraption in the woods to eat some meat, and I had then come out of the bushes, grabbed her and put her into a burlap bag, then taken her to a strange place, where she was held down and examined closely for sex and age, by strange beings she did not know who clipped something white onto one of her wings and then tossed her into the air, allowing her escape. Now she saw this same creature (me) offering her and him the absolute best food she could think of; it had to be a trick again.

She, as a raven and as any sentient being, is more conscious and cautious of something that could kill versus that which merely stimulates the palate. Every time she saw a raven—especially her mate—be lured by that being (me!) associated with that memory, her fear would automatically be triggered and communicated to her mate—and thus Goliath (who knew nothing of it given his opposite experience of being loved and catered to since he was still a pin-feathered nestling). And so, my friend parted from me. But that was likely not the end.

One day a neighbor and friend, Wallis Tyler, arrived at my camp with a badly injured raven he had seen being attacked by big black birds in dense bushes along the nearby highway. It was a pitiful sight, as the assailants had concentrated their attack on the head. It did not seem wild and took food from my hand, but lived only three or four days before I buried it.

I DON'T KNOW how ravens identify each other, but they do. What is perhaps more amazing is that they can distinguish us as individuals also, apparently at least in part by the face. Wild ravens that would flee from people from a distance in the wild soon fed almost at my feet in the aviary where I met them daily after I had captured them. Anyone else who might take my place, even when wearing my clothes, they avoided. How they identify each other seems more of a mystery, as to me they look too much alike to differentiate by their appearance. Behavior is, however, far more individual.

Ravens are playful; they routinely pull on the tail of a dog or eagle, as though for fun when they are young. Adult ravens who have never seen a string in their life will pull up a piece of meat suspended by a yard-long string by one loop at a time, carefully holding each successive loop with a foot. Though totally inexperienced, they will also pull *down* on a piece of string as well to make meat come up over a barrier if otherwise not available. They fly off immediately if handed a piece of meat with or without string, but not if it is attached. If two strings are close together, they pull up only the one to which the food is attached; they are logical. Like us, they have culture: What one raven learns is passed on to others by example.

I LEARNED MUCH from these birds during what I call "the raven years." It had been made possible by the dream of a childhood living in the forest with a crow. It happened, and many people generously took part to reveal the nature of that amazingly intelligent creature of our Northern Forests. The raven would have also sparked the imaginations of those who depended on "him" for their lives in ages past. Humankind was coeval with the raven ever since *Homo sapiens* ventured out of Africa and then traveled everfarther north until they could go no farther. But always, always the ravens would have been with us. Ravens always appeared from high in the sky; when they spotted caribou, they would lead humans to the herd, and after the kill, humans would make sure there was plenty left for the ravens. The vastness of the sky was no limit to this joyful exuberance, nor the coldest nights all winter long, because the two-legged ones clad in fur were always there, and if not, they followed them as they would the other furred ones, the ones with antlers and four legs. Those with weapons worshipped the raven, as he was a sky being, one for whom neither cold, distance, speed, knowledge, nor even the sky itself were limits, whereas his meat providers were bound to the cold winter ground in deep snow and ice.

For me, the greatest raven satisfaction was finding scientific *proof* that they can think; by that I mean they are able to predict a future result without having inherited or learned the intermediary steps. I did a relatively simple series of experiments that anyone could have undertaken, as others had with bumblebees and spiders. They "came" to me simply by my closeness to the ravens. The first involved chunks of suet. When I gave one to jays or crows, they immediately pecked and hammered away, breaking off bite-sized pieces. But when I offered the same pieces to ravens—too large for them to carry off—they approached it differently. Instead of randomly pecking, they systematically carved a groove, much like we might slice off a manageable portion of cake or steak. That alone was intriguing, but the real test came with strings.

I took a piece of meat and suspended it about a yard below a horizontal perch. A young, recently fledged raven landed, looked down at it, and did nothing—except for the occasional impulsive attempt to snatch it midair, inevitably failing, as the meat was tugged from its bill. But an adult raven, one that I hand-raised and that had never seen food on a string, behaved differently. It landed, assessed the situation, then grasped the string, pulling it up, securing the looped section again in its claw, and reaching down for the next pull—repeating the process until the meat was within reach.

Did the raven "know" what it was doing? To test this, I hung two strings side by side, only one holding food. The adult raven looked down, selected the correct one, and pulled. Mistakes happened, but if the strings were too close and it grabbed the wrong one, it immediately corrected itself. Then I made the challenge more complex—rigging the setup so that pulling *down*, not up, was the way to retrieve the food. Impossibly counterintuitive? Not for the raven. When the string was arranged on the far side of a wire screen so that, from the bird's perspective, the string moved upward when pulled down, it still solved the problem—without trial and error. This was not rote learning; it was foresight.

The key observation in all of this was that my hand-raised birds were not simply executing instinctive behaviors like a machine following preprogrammed instructions. They were visualizing the result before acting. And that is the foundation of intelligence. However, it takes a great deal of evidence before one can confidently say that a behavior is rooted in thought. Instinct alone can produce astonishingly complex actions, just as a machine can perform incredible feats based on programming. But what I saw in ravens was something more—they were reasoning, problem-solving, and quite possibly imagining before they acted.

The implications are, I believe, awesome—because thinking is the main capacity generally assumed to set us apart from the "animals." It makes us all one, with or despite differences; it banishes the notion of they—other creatures—being things and hence inferior and expendable.

Nine

Mysteries of Porcupines and Spiders

It is variety that excites. And nature is inordinately more intricate than the human mind can even begin to perceive.

RAVENS IN WINTER, *1989*

THE PORCUPINE (*ERETHIZON DORSATUM*), ALSO called a "hedgehog," is, according to *The Mammal Guide*, by Ralph S. Palmer, "a large, stout, quilled rodent, with a small head, short legs, and stout tail." If you should ever consider living in the North Woods, you'll need to know more than the three pages devoted to the porcupine by Palmer, where you learn that "oval-to bean-shaped droppings about 5/8 in. long" and that when porcupines make love they have an elaborate courtship where the male "utters high falsetto sounds, approaches the female, rubs her nose, and showers her with urine."

I have rubbed noses, so to speak, with porcupines from nearly my first days in the Maine woods at age eleven, when I at once fell in love with them. First impressions are often forever, and mine of a porcupine perched on the thick branch of an oak tree about fifteen feet above my head is indelible. However, this creature didn't budge, staying motionless as if stuck there as a decoration.

My father found another one for me in the woods that spring. It was furry-fuzzy, as they are when born, not spiny-prickly as they become. It was quite large for a near-newborn rodent and precocial. At birth porcupines weigh about 8 percent of their mother's weight, compared with a human's near-6 percent, so this one was nearly a pound. A wooden crate served as its otherwise normal den under a hollow tree. I fed "Porky" raspberry stalks by hand, and "he" was nonchalant and accepting, but then trundled off and I never saw him again.

Porcupines are valuable animals because if you are lost and starving, you can always club one on the head with a stick, since they won't run away. At around age sixteen, I did just that, treating my two like-aged and like-minded but still skeptical buddies to a feast. It was wintertime in the snowy forest, and we warmed ourselves around our campfire while roasting the meat.

YEARS LATER, WHEN I was a student at the University of Maine in Orono, I read in Palmer's book, "I have eaten porcupine liver often; the meat, however, of a young one had a rather unpleasant taste." I don't recall the taste of liver versus other parts, but ours was no longer young, and one of my partners-in-feast later reminded me, "You got sicker than a dog." I may have volunteered that experience to my professor, Al Barden, because I got an A in the course, for effort. Since those days, porcupines and I have had a close association.

Porcupines are still a constant presence in the woods where I live. There's a porcupine that consistently uses a huge hollow yellow birch tree near my cabin as its home. Others den among rocks on the nearby ledges. In the winter they sally forth at night to their favorite feeding tree, primarily one of the rare hemlocks in the area. A single porcupine will dine on the same tree's branches and bark, leaves, and fruit night after night, and then year after year, until the tree dies from the delimbing. Then the porcupine picks another, adjacent tree. Each uses its own worn trail in the snow for back-and-forth travel to and from the den, and it climbs into the crown of the same tree, where it chews off branch after branch, dropping them onto the snow. It is difficult to see what, if anything, the porcupines may have eaten from those twigs, and so these fresh branches retain plenty of food as they fall from on high, a godsend to snowshoe hare and deer.

Hemlock can be their only food for months, or years, but then again, they eat the bark off almost anything. Up by the ledges they climb young beech trees and totally debark the top branches. In my maple grove, where I left several large beech trees, they ignore the maple yet have specifically taken the beech trees. One beech tree would provide them enough bark to last months, but instead they chew all around the base, without climbing the tree. It dies after a single porcupine meal, as they move on to the next. I have not seen the porcupines debark ash or birch or oak. But in the fall, when the acorns are ripe but before they are shed from the tree (and are then taken by bears, deer, turkeys, squirrels, and blue jays), the porcupines invariably climb to the top branches and snip off the acorn-bearing twigs to reach the acorns just as they ripen but before the tree sheds them.

Porcupines do not debark twigs or trunks of red and striped maple trees that when young are favorites of moose, whereas the sugar maples sometimes consumed by porcupines are generally not taken by moose. They also seem to have a taste for the exotic, as they famously chew on outhouse toilet seats, and as Palmer writes, also on "ax handles, canoe paddles and saddles." And he didn't even mention American chestnut trees and black locust, exotics for this forest, which they immediately picked when I planted them by my cabin, which then had to be guarded to outlive the porcupines' nightly incursions after one had located them.

It seems strange that this eat-anything rodent would pick out the one black locust tree in this forest or the two American chestnut trees out of the hundreds of thousands of other trees. But according to Dr. Uldis Roze, who has studied porcupines extensively in the Catskill Mountains, their eclectic diet resides in their taste for salt. That could potentially explain their taste for axe handles and toilet seats, yet nobody really knows.

For years porcupines spent their days in the dark, cave-like space under the floor of our cabin. Even now one uses my closest neighbor's subfloor gap for over-daying in the winter. I cross its tracks in the snow, fresh every day, always in the same path back and forth, out and back, to and from its hemlock tree in the evening and returning to the cabin. There are times, however, when a porcupine takes to wandering, which can happen in almost any season. You know it less by meeting them in the woods than by their carcasses along the roadside. Porcupines, unlike other animals that run away from a threat, generally stop, hunker down, and bristle up to show the quills on their back when threatened, which is not always an efficient defense when it comes to cars on the highway. Still, they are good survivors, since even while bearing only a single pup per year, if any, their population remains stable.

Much can be forgiven this chubby, clumsy, slow-moving but amazing herbivore that has evolved a good portion of its hairs into sharp darts that are pointed with microscopic barbs that point only one way upon impalement. These "quills" are loosely attached at the base, and if a tip penetrates a predator's skin it has but one way to go when it is agitated by a paw, and that is decidedly not in the reverse direction because of a sharp hook on the tip. Most potential wild predators, such as foxes, coyotes, and bears, likely know this, derived through generational knowledge. But domestic dogs generally have to learn it the hard way, and after one encounter they either avoid porcupines ever after or are so angered (if they had been fortunate to have been rescued) to attack all the harder the next time they find one. Our Australian sheepdog, Towhee, was of the first kind, and her trauma in the middle of the night fell mostly on us, her trusted friends.

One might think that the porcupines' evolved defense is impregnable. Only two wild predators that I know of have a successful porcupine-eating strategy: the mountain lion and, locally in New England, the fisher, a barely fifteen-pound weasel relative. I have only once come upon a recent kill scene: a porcupine had been under a brush pile, squeezed in apparently to protect itself from all sides, but the fisher had found a vulnerability and approached its intended victim at the head end. The porcupine was squeezed into the brush and could no longer turn around to use its lethal weapon—its muscular, thrashing, quill-studded tail. The fisher attacked by repeatedly jumping at its face, until its victim became incapacitated and could be turned over to expose the soft underbelly.

The porcupine attacks no one unless attacked. However, it does require us to have a defensive strategy to have a good relationship with it as a neighbor. One's garden, for example, is a porcupine's cornucopia of exotic fare, perhaps even more desired than the edge of a toilet seat, an axe handle, or a saddle. And their raids always occur at twilight or at night.

Once, when I had cultivated a plot of blackberries, I found an entire patch gone by dawn. This was before the plants had even bloomed. I then surrounded the garden with a five-foot-high wire mesh fence. All went well for a couple of years. Then, from one evening to the next day, half of the bushes were snipped off. What remained was flattened, and most of the stalks were missing. Porcupines can climb fences, and I had again underestimated their tastes and capability.

My neighbors, Jeff and Sheila Yates, in the woods on nearby Cherry Hill, were less worried about blackberry vines than about their pickup truck. I knew something was up when I visited them and noticed the bottom of the vehicle skirted with chicken wire. I guessed why right away. They'd had a regular night visitor, although not known about it for quite some time. All they knew for sure was that their truck would not start. The problem was traced to insulated electrical wires that had been chewed in the truck's understory. Exotic automobile parts are hard to find in the North Woods, except maybe by a porcupine, although how, why, and what for, like much of the porcupine psyche, remain a mystery.

Porcupines belong, like us, to the highest order of animals— the mammals—of which we humans all agree we are the most innovative, smartest, perhaps specifically chosen by God to run the world, if not up, then at least down. And this categorization is most easily done by counting the number of legs—the fewer the better. No animal has reached the epitome of us, at two, right up there with birds, but after the four-legged animals, insects are next with six, with spiders close behind with eight, then crustacea, centipedes, and last but not least, millipedes.

I don't understand why a centipede, who uses its legs to walk, and then only slowly, requires so many, but at least the crustacea use two of theirs for crushing and biting. These are not necessarily complex maneuvers, but I believe they have reached all-time sophistication (for an arthropod) in spiders. I'd never really seen how some build their webs, catch their food in them, and make a safe receptacle for carrying perhaps hundreds of their eggs and progeny all at once.

Building webs is of course what spiders are best known for, not for having a lot of legs for running. Building webs is what one of my favorite species does every year at strategic fly-catching spots in and around my cabin. I'd spent a year previously trying to learn their secrets and can say I made discoveries about these barn spiders, already well known from *Charlotte's Web*, a famous book by E. B. White that has a lot to say about a talking one. I'd have preferred White to show what spiders *really* do, not what we might dream they do or what people might like to hear about them.

But there were, like every year, a spider or two at every other of my windows. And they were, as of yet, not going anywhere. They were there to catch the mostly absent (this year) flies, but there *were* some bees outside on the goldenrod. Might the spiders like them, too? If so, what would the bumblebees *do* about it?

I'd first seen a spider's web and then forgotten about it, because it had been nearly invisible: Despite its seventeen inches in diameter, it was hidden under the top frame of my back door, spreading only about three inches in front of the glass plate in the upper part of the door frame. This web had twenty-three spoke threads radiating from its center, analogous to the spokes of a wheel. Those threads were held in place by fifteen circular threads, so there were about 345 touchpoints. Curiously, at the touchpoints the threads did not just touch: They *held together.* Yet the spider on touching the web did not ever stick to it. Plus, the more than twenty spokes from the center of the web extended past it to the spider's attack point and onto the door frame beyond.

I had, of course, seen these webs here often, but had not thought it noteworthy to sit and watch. I knew that any one of these spiders could spend days on end without moving even one of its eight legs. But seeing one, on a rainy day, two yards directly in front of me, every thread exposed and easily visible by the water droplets on it, made a difference. By its size I could tell that the occupying spider was several years of age, though not yet old, as I inferred from previous years having overwintered several in a cage in a cellar that I'd held as residents indoors on my window during previous summers.

To see how making and operating a spider web is done is not like watching a soccer player trying to score a goal. This is rarer and much more complicated and dramatic. The spider may have to wait days and does not budge until the prey is *in* the net, when the potential prey's escape attempts send vibrations along a thread that alerts the spider hiding in its lair above by jiggling a leg or two, its signal to rush down for the kill. An orb-weaver spider's threads of web are thin enough for the prey not to notice, but strong enough to hold it and the spider in a tussle—between a meal for the spider, likely its first in weeks, and the life of the intended meal. The spider in the tussle wraps his prey in sticky thread, shot out from glands at its rear end while it rotates the prey and nonstop exudes more sticky thread.

I wanted to see the nuances of the spider's skills in action, and not getting a bee right away, I managed to catch a dragonfly, which I tossed into the web. For a few seconds this larger-than-spider potential prey held still. But the spider, then using its first pair of legs, pulled on the web, causing the potential prey to jiggle and thus also the threads holding it and connecting to the spider, who then shot out from its lair and down to the dragonfly. In seconds, the spider had twirled multiple threads issued from its rear end around the dragonfly. Once securely held, the spider then turned it round and round while at the same time shooting out from its rear end what looked like sheets of threads that were wrapping its prey reminiscent of an Egyptian mummy. It then adroitly detached this now-bound prey from the web tangle by somehow cutting a thread here or there until the victim was then attached by only a single short thread to its left hind leg. Then, in no great hurry, the spider ambled back up to its lair and pulled its prey up behind it, dangling from one leg by that single thread.

Once tucked back into its window frame lair, the spider casually turned around and bit into its tightly bound victim. It held still for a minute or so killing it, and then again bit in, presumably injecting digestive juices into the fly. After four hours or so, the spider dropped (by cutting the threads by biting) the dry remnants of that dragonfly and tiny white poop specks later.

I doubt the spider had identified its prey by sight, because it had responded to its escape struggles: Whenever the dragonfly stopped struggling, the spider shook the web, and the vibrations created by its bounces and the fly's renewed struggles informed the spider of what was still on the lines, and where. The spider had known it was potential prey and not a stray leaf in the web because the dragonfly had by its movements responded, sending vibrations back up the web. (I tested the spider a day later by tossing it bits of twig. The spider then jiggled the web, but there was no response, and so it stayed unmoved in its lair.)

The web was a mess after the capture, but no matter how little or how badly the web was damaged in the daytime, it was always brand new by dawn. In a month there was only one morning when the web was as if ripped to shreds, perhaps by a huge moth that night. It was a surprise to see the web still torn at dawn, the spider not having repaired the web. The web remained that way all day. The next dawn, though, it was once again an intact superweb, but the threads were now spaced more closely together, at forty or forty-five threads.

It seemed a marvel to me how the spider could manage to produce the exquisite precision of the web, requiring the coordination of eight multijointed legs working in concert on the numerous threads and with no apparent visual aid. How could it get the thread spacing so precisely? How could it triangulate to place a web practically anywhere, as the placement of other webs suggested?

We dismiss the precision skill by calling it "instinct," an inherited behavior. But even if so, why does that make it less amazing than our flexible and variable human behavior? And just how flexible are we? If we are kind, understanding, and skilled, do we care if it turns out that our behaviors are based on learning facilitated by innate tendencies? The spider had shown incredible behavior applied with discretion. Might there be more? What if the prey is a wasp, hornet, or bee that can defend itself and kill with a sting?

I needed more testing and decided to give this spider a more challenging prey, a bumblebee, but first tossed a smaller bee, a honeybee, into the web. The bee put up a buzz, and the web jiggled and vibrated as expected. But this time, instead of the usual quick response, the spider desisted, at least for a while, and the bee, after hitting the web, stopped as if dead. Nothing happened, until after a while the bee slowly started to struggle using its legs only, in an apparent effort to scrape off the sticky threads. The spider then, hesitatingly, very *slowly* descended into the web, stopped, shook the web with its front legs, causing the bee to jiggle slightly, thus vibrating the web, and that gave the spider a clearer fix on the bee's location, and it then quickly found and bound it in silk. With one strand attached to the end of the prey's (again) *left* hind leg, the spider sallied up the web to its lair with its bound captive.

My subsequent staged spider-honeybee contests indicated mutual tactics. As in any game where one wins and the other loses, sometimes it is the other way around. For the most part, when I tossed bees into the web, they froze, although they were highly excited, since they showed very fast abdominal breathing movements, proof that (given my decades-earlier study of bee physiology) their flight muscles were working hard to stay flight ready. Meanwhile, the spider did not budge until, after many minutes, the bee did start struggling to extricate itself. The spider then started to slowly leave its lair and jiggle the web, as if for a test. The bee then invariably stayed stock-still, and it became what looked like a waiting game. Eventually, most of the honeybees I tried had time enough to extricate themselves and flew off unharmed. So I decided to test this spider with a bumblebee.

Bumblebees are most readily seen in the fall on the goldenrod bloom, and of these the orange-belted (*Bombus ternarius*) workers were available this year. Each so-called "worker" is a sterile female offspring of the queen (there are no male bumblebees around until late fall). Since spring the workers had been raised on a diet that stunts their growth and precludes them from ever having sex, but they look identical to the queen except for their smaller size, which is, however, almost *twice* that of a honeybee worker. As I approached the spider web with a very active bumblebee in a jar, I found the spider as usual tucked up in her lair and out of sight in a crack above my door. Hitting the web, the bumblebee instantly played dead; she showed neither leg nor wing motion but made very rapid and deep breathing movements of her abdomen. This meant she was pumping air into her flight muscles *to prepare or be ready for flight*, which requires contracting them at some sixty or so times per second. But with the wings not engaged to move, the bee looked dead, though she was operating like the pistons of a car engine in idling mode. So she appeared to be dead to the spider, but was in fact hugely alive and flight capable at any fraction of a second, if she were free.

The spider didn't budge, because it would not have been able to locate the bee as long as she didn't vibrate any thread with her long legs or wings. I waited and waited for the spider to make a move. Five minutes . . . then ten. . . . Nothing changed, until finally, using one of its legs, the spider yanked on a thread, jiggling the web as spiders do, to wiggle what *may* be in the web, and from the return pulses of the bouncing bee, to determine her location.

The yanking of the elastic threads of the web by the spider caused the bee to bounce up and down a bit, enough to alert the spider and allow it to get a fix on the bee's location. *Slowly* now, in almost a creep, the spider then descended from its lair down into the web. The bee, however, apparently "knew" what was happening, because the rate of her abdominal breathing vibrations, which had declined, now suddenly speeded up—she was revving up her flight muscle contractions, causing the required pumping motions of the abdomen for the oxygen required for breathing; she was scared.

The spider then very slowly approached the sitting bee, and when near, it finally extended one of its legs, touched her, and almost simultaneously shot out silk from its rear-end spinnerets while at the same time rotating the webbed-in bee, using several of its legs to spin it while it continued to hang onto the web. In mere seconds, the bee was silk-wrapped, but not in the usual single-strand *web* silk, but in a multistrand silk looking again like the white sheet on a mummy. I saw no more movement from the bee. The spider then held it at leg's length, bit it, and sauntered leisurely up into its lair, pulling the wrapped bee up by a *single* thread, held by a left hind leg.

Apparently, bees and spiders both have programmed responses; as the spiders evolve a better trap, the potential prey evolves capacity to oppose it. I stayed away from the literature, letting original observations be my guide, but when I did finally Google this spider, I was surprised to find that what I read was opposite to what I routinely saw: This spider did not, as was stated in Google, consume its web at night and build a new one in the daytime. By contrast, in the absence of prey, it descended into the web only after dark, when it meticulously repaired its web. However, some of the baby spiders stayed in their webs all day. Their webs were miniatures of the adult version in shape and number of threads, and some were so close to an adult's web that one may wonder whether they might be captured and consumed.

My pseudo-Charlotte was likely close to a decade old. Natural spider lifetimes of a decade are, I suspect, conservative. Few of us stay in one place over many seasons keeping track of an individual spider.

At the beginning of fall, most of the spiders' insect prey are in winter quarters, and all the bumblebee workers, males, and acting queens have died, with the new queens underground. I look forward to seeing my "Charlotte" next year at the same exact spot. It is now deer rutting time, when friends and I traditionally start the hunt for our venison, as regular as any spider and bumblebee queen go underground to hibernate. Deer hunting does not match their patience, skill, and endurance, but it is a good time, maybe the last before the snow flies, to get intimate contact with the North Woods at their best, loaded with memories of the golden past.

Part IV

Remembering

Ten

Nothing Is Ever Noticed Except in the Memory of Connections

A life is ultimately not philosophy. It is specifics. . . .

THE SNORING BIRD, 2007

AT THE AGE OF EIGHTY-FOUR, I STILL REMEMBER what life felt like when I was fourteen on my first deer hunt. I loved to hunt—beetles and caterpillars for myself, although not so much the ichneumon wasps for my entomologist father. Neighbor Floyd Adams and his boys Jimmy, Billy, and Vernon taught me how to hunt for wild bee trees. Passion for the hunt came from deep within me, likely an instinct inherited from our beginnings long before we were humans. The appetite is surely genetic as well as learned culturally, and it is passed on that way, too.

Another neighbor, Phil Potter, instigated my first deer hunt on a morning just before school. He loaned me his .30-30 Winchester rifle, which I later inherited from him and still own. I'd gone into our woods at dawn, "got" my deer before breakfast, and announced the feat to my class, where volunteers offered to help me drag it out later that day.

Twenty or so years after this first deer, when my nephew Charlie was also high school age, I took him for *his* first hunt. At noon we perched on a boulder under the old beech trees up on the top of the hill at Houghton Ledges (near where I met the ravens). As we ate our lunch, a buck with a big rack appeared through the beeches as in a dream. We both lifted our rifles and shot at once.

We've been deer hunting every November since, me with the same .30–30 Winchester, Charlie with something more modern. Over the years I have grown more ambivalent about hunting and can take it or leave it, perhaps because I am less moved by passion than by logic, and my logic says that a North Woods without wolves or their equivalents will result in a deer population explosion that will kill the forest, a forest I love with all that is in it.

In 2023, Charlie came up from Pennsylvania, as he does every year, and with miraculous luck, patience, and good judgment, shot a deer on our first day out. But it was a poorly aimed shot; wounded, the deer ran off, which is always a wrenching experience. Moments after the shot, we heard a raven call, and it continued its commotion from where the deer was heading, a densely forested balsam fir thicket. The raven called again and again, and it led us to where the deer lay. Charlie and I left the raven, and later coyotes, ample reward before continuing the mile-long deer drag back to camp.

Charlie then headed south after what was an exceptionally short deer season for him, but on the last day of deer hunting season, a month later, I decided to give it another proverbial shot. I chose a large pine tree, one I'd often thought might be ideal to climb, and sat on a high branch and waited, enjoying the view and any and all wildlife that might come by. I'd seen a fresh deer track earlier in the already available snow. I was especially keen to observe birds for my current project, a study of mixed-species flocks in winter. This pine had unusually thick limbs, and I could climb to any height, bringing along my rifle, as well as a pen and paper for taking notes.

High in the branches I faced a gorgeous panorama—giant pines, maples, and now over a thousand young American chestnut trees, offspring of those I planted forty years ago. I did not want to see the chestnut seedlings eaten or browsed off by either deer or hare. I needn't have worried about hares. I hadn't seen one here for years, although they used to be common after the hayfields and pastures first returned to woods. I thought I'd seen the last hare then, when the brush had turned to forest, but last year one appeared directly under my cabin window and died there overnight, so I suspect there had been a disease outbreak, since it had now been several years since I heard the two "rabbit" hunters' beagles bark. The pair would ask to hunt on my land, and they always got my permission, as I do not own the rabbits or the deer any more than the soil or the air.

Facing west from my perch in the pine, I patiently followed the ever so slowly moving sun, heading on its downward journey. Soon, freezing from the lack of activity, I was shivering like a late autumn maple leaf in the breeze.

Finally, a bird came by, my first and only brown creeper so far this autumn. It landed less than a yard away near the bottom of a thick Balsam fir tree and then ascended, taking its quick, typical short hops.

I kept waiting for deer as the air grew colder and the urge to quit grew stronger, but I thought, "What if, after all this preparation, a deer comes by minutes after I have given up and left?," so I stayed, violently shivering. The sun was getting lower, and

I promised myself I could make it to four thirty, which I did, then trotted happily back to the cabin in the dark to get warm.

Only later did I realize I had experienced something very unusual while perched in that pine . . . something I had not even been thinking about . . . the *silence.*

There were no flocks of chickadees, gold- and purple finches, pine siskins, pine grosbeaks, redpolls, or the occasional evening grosbeaks in the nearby forest on the conifers. Nor had there been many of the common warblers months earlier. When I thought of such routine outings in the past, going back decades, there were always birds. I'd cross paths with the black-capped chickadees that were so common I tended to take them for granted. Each flock would be accompanied by a pair of red-breasted nuthatches, perhaps a white-breasted one also, a downy woodpecker, usually several golden-crowned kinglets, and perhaps a brown creeper. Where were they? Where was their song?

No birds. *Silence.* It took a while for it to really sink in, because I'd not felt it while perched in the pine. Now I was reminded that *nothing is ever noticed except in reference to the past and the effect of memory on it.*

A young deer hunter just starting out after me here, who had the same experience as mine today, would not have noticed this. They would have left with a very different picture, thinking it all "normal."

RARE SEASONAL EVENTS may seem trivial because most trees, bees, and birds that depend on them can recover. Yet, each event bequeaths a legacy.

The seasons and weather are tightly linked, with weather resulting mainly from Earth's tilt in reference to the sun as Earth makes its orbit, and with the seasons being four consecutive sub-units of that time. The amount of illumination reaching Earth varies—the least reaching Earth during winter and the most during summer—with the seasons in regions toward the North Pole exactly opposite the seasons toward the South Pole. If it were not for that tilt, there would be no seasons, and much of life would be extraordinarily different. Days in winter of no sun alternating with summers of little night has a huge effect on tree growth and hence the forest. Having spent one summer on Ellesmere Island, near the North Pole, I recall only one species of tree there, a willow that barely reached an inch above the ground, but its roots underground were likely as old as any in the Northern Forest, where trees typically reach ten feet or so.

Aside from the systematic and predictable climate changes caused by Earth's axis of rotation in its annual journey around the sun, and also the very unpredictable events of volcanic eruptions and giant meteor impacts that created havoc to life on Earth, such as the dinosaurs' extinction. Each and every climatic event can be a lesson.

I will never forget when here in northern New England about twenty years ago an "ice storm" hit suddenly in January. My students and I happened to be at the cabin for our Winter Ecology course. It had been a cold night, and the woods were like a deep freeze when it started to rain, and temperatures dropped. All trees became encased in ever-thickening layers of ice and provided an immediate lesson of trees' adaptations to the Northern Forest. Most trees remained standing, having by then shed their leaves as an adaptation for such a potentially killing calamity, although many still suffered damage, depending on structure: Large trees with large branches reaching too far laterally had them bent and broken because of the leverage of weight at their ends. White and black ash have compound leaves of about six to eight leaves connected to one unit that is shed, thus reducing twigs that would otherwise be needed to hold leaves. Having more of the limbs growing vertically and reducing branching promoted more water running off rather than collecting on as ice.

Birches, given their numerous twigs, soon collected ice, but the twigs are thin and yielded, hanging down so that water ran off and there was less surface for water to collect on and freeze. But most impressive were the balsam firs and the spruces, true northern trees. They ended up with no damage at all. With their cone shapes and limbs that taper from trunk to branch tip, they simply ended up with their limbs bending down onto each other, producing a large cone where snow or water runs off to all sides. Thus, while huge deciduous trees with large, thick lateral branches were succumbing, these conifers were unaffected.

The ice storm in midwinter occurred within two or three years of a snowstorm in spring, right after the deciduous trees had extended their leaves from their buds. The result was near that of the ice storm in winter. I especially remember the many young trees bent over and broken, having reached too high, but not able to balance much load. The large deciduous trees lost horizontal branches. There were, however, differences in the number of frost-bitten leaves and in twig and flower growths. None of the beech has in many years now produced flowers, although some adjacent tree species at the same time produced bumper fruit and seed crops.

But unusual effects can become usual. Climate has a profound effect on all of life, especially that of birds, bees, and people.

No animals are so spectacularly seasonal as insects in the Northern Forest. Most of us who venture into the wild are of course familiar with those that take our blood, such as the blackflies in early spring. The ticks (though they are not insects, but classed with the arachnids, or spider family) are close behind. But the horseflies and deerflies take the late summer shift, along with the eye flies in the muggy days of late August. They are so tiny that they would dehydrate in minutes if encountering air that is not saturated with water, and they try to save themselves from that fate by aggressively flying into our eyes for moisture, which is all the more difficult for us to fight off than any of the previous, which one can swat or keep at bay with various toxic ointments. The midges that fly at night are even smaller but no less merciless.

For cicadas, seasonality has evolved to extremes. They do not follow an annual life cycle like most creatures. Instead, theirs is variable, spanning years. Unlike insects (or any animals) with annual cycles, where each generation completes its development within a single year, periodical cicadas remain underground for over a decade before emerging in massive, synchronized numbers. Some species of cicada appear every seventeen years, while others follow a thirteen-year cycle. Varying seasons of their absence and unavailability is likely an antipredator adaptation. When the noisy adults emerge from the ground, they ideally attract mates, of which there will be many, rather than predators that would eat them.

———————

IN THE LAST forty years at my cabin, I have thus seen other seasons—aside from those determined by month, year, or decade—such as those of a moth and its ichneumon wasp parasite, perhaps an example of what Rachel Carson meant when she wrote in *Silent Spring* in 1962: "The balance of nature is not a status quo; it is fluid, ever-shifting, in a constant state of adjustment. Man, too, is part of the balance."

Back in the 1950s, there was a big scare in Maine over the spongy (gypsy) moths (*Lymantria dispar*) because this species has the capacity to multiply fast, but as it turns out, so do some of their ichneumon "parasites." My father, one of the rare specialists conversant with the thousands of species, was thus closely acquainted with the renowned entomologist Lincoln Brower. The Maine Department of Agriculture was heavily into spraying DDT to kill off the gypsy moth plagues that were defoliating trees, and it was noted that when they killed a few, they kept on defoliating and killing more, so the administrators decided to nip these pests' progress in the bud before they eliminated the northern hardwood forests. Dr. Bower helped me get a summer job up in Aroostook County, in the North Woods of Maine, to try to find any flare-ups of the moths there. I got issued a truck and a huge number of tubular traps, each equipped with a wick dipped in the female gypsy moth sex scent; chemists had identified its chemical structure and could produce it in large amounts. The traps were also equipped with a sticky glue, so the moths would get stuck inside on gluey paper rather than on a female moth they'd perceived "calling." I was religious in my job, working each day and all day, except twice taking weekends off to hitchhike the one hundred miles home to be with family and farm.

My result was good. I didn't catch a single moth, proof that Aroostook County was spongy moth free and didn't need to get sprayed. At the same time, Rachel Carson's world-famous *Silent Spring* was published. It reported that spraying DDT was causing the imminent extinction of the peregrine falcon, among other things, so DDT spraying was stopped.

Decades later, driving back and forth between Vermont and Maine in 1985, I encountered all the oak trees bared by gypsy moth caterpillars near Bethel, Maine. A couple of years later the moths had, after reaching peak population densities, become ideal fodder for the moth parasites, predators, and diseases, and the whole population crashed—all died.

Pesticides have never been sprayed on my forest. And I have found the very typical unambiguous and easy-to-identify spongy moth egg clumps (of hundreds of eggs each), but only two or three in all my decades here. Yet, I have not seen one moth, ever, though there could be at any time. I know why: Ichneumon wasps and other parasites continue to multiply faster than *they* do. Nature knows best if one gives it a chance.

Eleven

Red Leaves of Summer

Contrasts pique interest, in bird and man.

ONE WILD BIRD AT A TIME, 2016

ALMOST SUDDENLY BY JULY EVERY TWIG ON EVERY tree in my forest has finished growing its annual several inches or feet and has put on a load of now fully grown leaves. There is then scarcely a sunfleck on the forest floor, and a path through the woods is like a tunnel, even on a mountainside, until you reach the ledges on top from where the view reveals an endless blanket of brilliant green reaching unbroken in all directions, with the only variation perhaps a mountaintop or a beaver bog. It is a scene like those the early settlers in Maine experienced two centuries ago—and then eliminated much of it by axe and fire, to grow their crops and raise their livestock. But the New England forest has come back, a vast multilayered solar energy collector, growing and powering its life by nuclear fusion reactions in the sun. But in the Northern Forest the effects most desired seldom come soon enough.

At midsummer, when baby birds are fledging, when the spring flowers are shutting down and producing their fruit and seeds, the shade-loving or -tolerating ferns, mosses, and lycopods are still brilliant green and will remain so all winter. Scattered fresh green leaves are still dribbling onto the ground, the leftovers that highly camouflaged caterpillars are snipping off.

The phoebe's fledging and the red leaves on now shaded maple branches were a reminder of summer winding down, although lantern beetles' brilliant on-off flashing was still on at night along with the hermit thrush's languid melodious piping. The inexorable progression of pink fireweed was quickly followed by the goldenrods, and then the purple asters shortly before the leaf fall, when the hermit thrush became silent and was fattening up, preparing for its flight to winter in southern South America.

Although of great consequence to the caterpillars, the selective leaf loss is now of less cost than benefit to the trees. But then to my great surprise I found green *branches* down on the ground, including fresh live oak limbs of up to an inch thick. They had been neatly cut off in what looked like a slice so smooth one could only mimic it with a sharp knife. And this was not mere brush. These were full branches from the treetops of both red oak and rock or sugar maple. I was astonished, not knowing what had happened, but realizing there would be a story behind this, as these twigs from high in the tree lacked distinctive tooth-chew patterns such as of a rodent; they were perfectly smooth cuts sliced through. I could not resist taking measurements of at least one specimen to convince myself it was real.

The perfectly fresh oak branch was 1.6 yards long and an inch thick with four side branches. It held a total of 291 fresh leaves. Oak is tough. Live branches do not drop cut off on their own, and I tried to sleuth the thing out, starting at the cut end that showed five growth rings cut to be perfectly visible and at a right angle to the twig's length. I snipped off a section of the end, leaving it on my desk for later scrutiny and sketching. The next day, to my great surprise, I saw at that end a pile of fine wood powder. Something *live* was inside the wood releasing the powder at an exit hole that I could not see, but work with a sharp knife revealed a tunnel within the center of the branch. It led down to a .78-inch-long and .086-inch-thick yellowish-white long-horned beetle grub, with dot-sized deep brown mandibles. How such a tiny soft grub could chew through a fresh solid oak branch of such tough hardwood—a challenge for me with a sharp bush cutter and knife—seemed a marvel. Did it go to all the trouble to cut off the branch so it could then spend the winter beneath the snow in a not-so-cold subnivean environment?

It was not too early to prepare for winter, and I was preparing for not being bodily snow covered myself, as was almost every other living thing. The bumblebee drones, though, were still lounging on the goldenrod flowers, but they had no need for finding winter quarters. They were now all near the end of their lives, according to their annual colony cycle, when only the few new queens for next year would be mating, then preparing for winter by burrowing themselves into the ground to hibernate the next eight months in relative safety, provided they are out of reach of shrews, mice, and moles. Was this beetle larva doing the same kind of preparation for winter to survive freezing and predation?

I had by this time been, along with the bear that had been tempted to reach the bird feeder by my window, harvesting an unusual crop of blackberries and blueberries, preserving them not as fat, but as is, in my solar-energy-powered freezer. After I had extricated the beetle larva, I put it into a jar along with a short section of its oak branch and deposited the jar into the freezer. To my surprise it again chewed an almost microscopic pinhole through the bark.. I shall keep it now, hoping to see a beetle by springtime, remembering what it did to endure. But the animal itself could not have known, a reminder that the same applies to all and to some extent even to us.

SOME YEARS AGO, I discovered bright red leaves on the red maple trees (*Acer rubrum*) around my cabin in July. I'd assumed all the leaves would be green then, as are those of all the rest—the sugar maple, ash, beech, and chestnut. But only very specific leaves were red, and after a while I could predict which ones would turn red, and when. Maple twigs put on leaves in pairs, one to each side of a twig, and successive pairs in opposite directions. But only the first two pairs of topmost leaves of the very young trees were red, and only if those were in direct sunlight.

I was surprised and embarrassed on first noticing what I'd undoubtedly seen over a respectable lifespan, but still had never *noticed*. Everyone knows that all the thousands of leaves of the *whole* red maple tree turn from startling green in summer to bright red in the fall. We are taught it is the red pigment (anthocyanin) that protects the leaf from sunburn and that shows up only after all the green photosynthetic molecules have been broken down to then reveal these previously present red pigments. The leaves of young red maple trees in the shade, though, were certainly all fully green, not having a hint of red. But if so, why specifically do the younger leaves produce the red in the sun, when to grow they need to catch the most solar energy with the green chlorophyll?

That July I found something similar at a huge serviceberry (*Amelanchier*) tree. Scattered under it were hundreds of recently shed bright orange leaves, while the crown was a thick layer of green foliage; only a few orange leaves were still attached to the *low* shaded branches. Routinely now seeing *topmost* leaves of baby maples bright red was a surprise, but then finding a patch of ground in July strewn with red maple leaves that had been shaded made it even more so. They stimulated a fresh look at more leaves, especially when I found fresh *green* leaves strewn as if discarded on the ground everywhere, and these were not those showing caterpillar feeding damage.

Picking them up for a close look, I found that every one of them—sometimes a dozen under a single tree—had *not* been cast off by the tree in the usual way, at the usual junction between the end of the petiole and the twig. Instead, these whole leaves had been detached by an apparent cut *through* the petiole. Maple leaves have conspicuously long petioles, and these had been severed at almost any place along their full length. I'd never before seen or heard of anything like this, even though years earlier I had discovered that some (large) caterpillars, after finishing a meal on a leaf (generally at night) and then hiding from bird predators, go through the considerable trouble of chewing through the petiole to get rid of the leaf that would not be used. But here there was no sign of any caterpillar damage on any leaf, nor of a caterpillar, either. Would the *tree* get rid of its perfectly good leaves? And if it did, wouldn't it be by the usual mechanism of enzymes dissolving the tissue holding the leaf at the junction where the petiole attaches to the twig?

To be sure that the tree was not just dispensing leaves that were in some way faulty or superfluous, I enclosed a half dozen leafy branches in black opaque garbage bags to see if the tree would then shed those shaded leaves. The result? A week later almost all the leaves still held solidly to their twigs. Except one, where I found two tiny white aphids on the petiole. Had this common sap-sucking insect punctured the leaf to access its liquid nutrients in the petiole, rather than puncture the leaf surface? It could be a good strategy, because petioles are the conduit of nutrients into and out of the leaf, and thus for a sucking insect it may be a good place to tap, like us tapping into the trunk of a maple tree for sap, and so it would be to the tree's advantage to discard a leaf that an aphid is parasitizing, especially when it's a rapidly reproducing resident.

Meanwhile, in the neighboring bogs, many red maples that grow there also turn red, a whole month before those in this forest. I cut the midrib of some leaves, as it functions not only as support but also as a water and nutrient channel: as I'd guessed, they soon turned red. But why change color at all, as if to announce senescence?

Already in mid-September, swamps light up in bright reddish purple, standing out like oases in the solid green of surrounding forest, and by mid-October, the red swamp maples are leafless. Upslope, however, at elevations above a thousand feet, most are still partially leafed out. Frosty nights and clear days are thought to "bring out" the colors, although leaf shedding is likely influenced by photoperiods and circannual biorhythms, which trigger the production of abscission enzymes that dissolve the cell layers that adhere the leaves to the twig and detach leaves from their branches. The mix of cues generating colors may be difficult to determine, given the huge variability from one tree leaf to another, seasonal change, soil, altitude, weather, and individually specific genetics.

Of all the trees in the Northern Forest, the red maple is the most variable in color. One red maple in my clearing turns mostly lemon yellow, another crimson, and still another orange. However, most red maples are indeed red, true to their name, and most senescing sugar maples turn a rich yellow, although some individual trees of this species also turn red, and sometimes even purple. There is in most organisms no "best." It all depends on environment, which changes all the time.

In recent years, each tree in my clearing has assumed the same or similar *individual* tree-specific color every fall. Those of their kind in the surrounding forest appear variously colored in hues of red, purple, yellow, or pink. In contrast, the other three native maples—striped, mountain, and silver—all turn pale yellow before they brown. The striking differences between one tree kind and another, and often one leaf and another of the same kind, pose questions of how or why these color variations are possible and the cues that trigger them.

To probe what or if specific triggers might affect leaf senescence and color change in the red maple, I put some leaves to a test in mid-October. My subjects were still fully green leaves on twigs that would show their colors in about a week. I dipped the marked (with a thread on the petiole) leaves into either cold, warm, or scalding water, water saturated with salt, or an alcohol solution, and I cut the midrib of leaves about halfway along its length. Control leaves were dipped into water at air temperature.

The results were clear: The scalded leaf that was killed turned brown—up to the water contact dip line, where there was a tinge of bright green. The rest of the leaf turned a pale yellow, like the controls. The one dipped in alcohol solution showed no effect, except for a slight greening around the edges of the leaf. Physical damage that did not kill had little effect, and similar results came from examinations of caterpillar-damaged leaves, such as those eaten by leaf miners, the microcaterpillars that feed inside leaves rather than on them. Nor were they affected from myriad other organisms that chewed from the sides into the midrib, with its fluid transport pathways. Mechanical damage is apparently not the main cause of the biochemical changes for leaf color variation or for color patterns on the yellow background of senescing red maple leaves. However, sometimes an exception reveals much.

LIKE THE LEAVES of many other tree species—beech, American chestnut, birch, and larch—those of quaking aspen (*Populus tremuloides*) "always" turn golden yellow as they senesce before they fall. Unlike those of red maples, they are normally not marked with blotches and spots of different colors. However, a leaf miner moth, one who as a caterpillar specializes in feeding *within* the leaf tissue at the base of the petiole, leaves a conspicuous bright *green* area by the leaf petiole where it resides. The leaf area is not damaged, but is *prevented or delayed from senescing* to become yellow, unlike the rest of the leaf, suggesting that the moth produces an antiaging chemical that may keep it surrounded by food for a longer than normal duration. So, it can be seen as an insect's adaptation that reduces the leaves' "normal" rate of senescence and provides more nutrient to the occupants inside the leaf.

Most of the fall color display is due to three plant pigments in various combinations. The green of chlorophyll is the pigment that captures the sun's energy. But producing it, as with any molecule, requires an investment of energy. Plants, when they shed their leaves, recoup some of their investment by breaking down their chlorophyll into absorbable and reusable raw material.

This breakdown of the green pigment allows for the recovery of nitrogen and magnesium, to be available for use the next year, and their removal then reveals yellow and orange pigments (xanthophyll and carotenoids), which absorb the light energy that chlorophyll cannot absorb. These pigments reside in the chloroplast and, as antioxidant agents, may protect cells from oxygen—a highly reactive molecule—produced during photosynthesis.

Additionally, anthocyanins—the pigments that appear as red, purple, or blue—may be synthesized after chlorophyll is degraded and may have some unknown function, but are generally thought to serve as *sunscreens* and, like xanthophyll and carotenoids, provide an antioxidant defense against solar radiation. These red/purple/blue pigments are induced by cold nights and bright sunny days. They also make fruits visually conspicuous, attracting animals that then distribute the ingested plant seeds.

Early leaf fall costs the trees the intake of solar energy, but late leaf fall risks snow loading and can topple trees or tear off branches. The balance shifts with climate change, and global warming will predictably favor broad-leaved trees, such as beech and oak, as opposed to conifers, such as spruce and firs, that because they are conical can shed snow off their branches. But color as such makes practically no difference to trees after they are done with photosynthesis. Leaf color is a by-product of their previous physiological processes of growth and photosynthesis and the economy of resources for building their solar panels for the next year.

Twelve

A World of Our Making

Most of the lives around us go on unnoticed. They leave no records. We see only bits and pieces, and then only if we look very, very close-ly, or for very, very long. We have to decipher these other natives of the forest if we want to understand the landscape. A million scents that we never smell waft on the breezes; each of them has special meaning to some insect. If I chop this tree down in the summer, there will be hundreds of beetles of half a dozen species to smell it. They will come flying up against the wind and lay their eggs, which will soon turn into white grubs. Different kinds of wasps will then come to lay their eggs on the grubs, and woodpeckers will later feast on both. There are thousands of beetles of exquisite designs, and not a living person knows even so much as their names.

A Year in the Maine Woods, 1994

ANIMALS' PREPARATIONS FOR WINTER AND EVIDENCE of those preparations are centered on behavior. From my window every autumn I watch the resident chipmunks' apparent play—making burrows in the ground and under the woodshed and then repeatedly skipping back and forth all day to and from a nearby wild pin cherry tree, with cheeks stuffed, bulging full, hardly taking a break. Weeks later, after the snow is piled a yard deep and they've taken long naps, these ground squirrels occa-sionally awake for a snack and then take another week-long sleep or two or three, but come spring they pop back up and romp through the melting snow. Wood frogs nearly freeze into ice, their skin receptors triggering the release of adrenaline, which prompts the liver to convert glycogen into glucose, creating an antifreeze effect that protects their cells until the spring, when they thaw from that ultradeep sleep to sing and mate. It is the same old strategy, varying in one way or another for most of us, from bears to bumblebee queens.

The more we learn how amazingly every plant and animal adapts to living in the Northern Forest, the more they have reason to see us as deficient. It is no accident that come fall, even given the abundant supply of food at our local grocery stores, there is nevertheless a virtual migration of my fellow northerners to hurricane-prone Florida. I choose not to, but survive here wonderfully in the winter, only requiring a couple of axes, wedges, a chain saw or two (just in case one fails), a truck (or other vehicle), a gas generator, blankets, new thick clothes, boots, matches, a stove, coffee, and food either collected or grown here the previous summer or acquired from a thousand miles distant. More recently I also "need" a cell phone, a computer, and solar panels with eight batteries each that I can just barely lift, and which are useless in the winter. But I'm stuck. I have no migrating urge to South America.

Birds are the crystal-clear champions of the escape strategy to get to a better place. As early as August, the juvenile ruby-throated hummingbirds from this year's crop of always only two babies per nest are regulars, sucking up pure sugar water from my feeder. By late August they will be off to Texas and Louisiana and then fly over the Gulf of Mexico. Somehow, they make it back every summer, usually sucking up the sugar solution from my feeder within minutes after I hang it out in June. The sapsucker woodpeckers already arrive in time to tap sugar maple trees. They do not have to make it all in one flight, yet sandpipers have been radio-tracked flying nonstop for six days from northern Alaska to the Southern Hemisphere, thus staying in the warm in a, to them, continuous spring-summer. I admit to once going into a wood in a snow-storm to visit a neighbor and ending up, to my surprise, not rec-ognizing where I had gone. Lack of practice can be lethal. But of course, all birds have to do it right the first time, and not just over a quarter mile.

Weathering the seasons in place is highly recommended if you are used to chopping wood—and then staying by the fire in the daytime as well as at night.

WINTER, THE TIME of energy crunch, is when most life departs the Northern Forest, goes underground, and/or clumps up with others, and not always to mutual satisfaction. It can be lonely for us local human residents after the cottages around the lake empty, the loons, geese, and bald eagles have left, the local town bar at the Kawanhee Inn closes, and the tree swallows have flown thousands of miles south. The few painted and snapping turtles, frogs, and salamanders and the many insects are transformed into inert near-lifeless stages sequestered underground or underwater in brooks, ponds, and streams, and so there are seldom visitors to my cabin a half mile up a steep hill, given a merely foot-long-deep snow bar-rier in all directions.

Last autumn by far the most numerous winter visitors (becoming lodgers) were ladybird beetles. All summer they repro-duce in the surrounding forest, their larvae feeding on aphids in the foliage. By late summer, their larvae become winged adults, and on sunny days they start flying in, landing in the afternoons in droves onto the south-facing side of the cabin. From there they enter my cabin through cracks and crevices, and once inside they are not inclined to leave. In the evenings there is sometimes light at a bedside that attracts them. Almost always when indoors they get alarmed and release bad-smelling yellow droplets of predator repellant, fluid exuded at their leg joints. A few green lacewings used to come in too, but nothing compared to the cluster flies. One year I collected over nine cups of these flies, as noted in an earlier book, *A Year in the Maine Woods.* Now, many years later in the same woods, I've only *very* rarely seen even *one* of these flies. It bothers me a lot, but it is not from loneliness; I still have deer mice.

THIS LAST SPRING I had positive proof that not just one mouse was visiting me. Suddenly in the dark something dropped from the ceiling where quick skittering footsteps and buzzing had come from earlier, suggesting mice were nesting there. It was a pitch-dark night when something fell onto my face. A big bug? No. I reached up, and it was a young mouse. After that, the noise declined, then stopped after I set traps and caught mice, all eagerly received by the barred owl that had been hanging out in the white birch by my bird feeder, my main draw for always-welcomed feathered visitors.

This owl, however, was a new visitor compared to another a decade or so earlier that after several months came *every* day *and* night without fail (because I fed it *every* time), until it would dive from its favorite perch in the white birch tree by my door. It routinely took mice out of my hand and eventually dived at almost anything I offered. This new owl was still shy with me, but not afraid enough to stay away; it accepted my occasional gifts of mice. But when I ran out of mice, I found an owl pellet (a mass of the bones and furs of an owl meal) with the skull of a shrew in it. Shrews, smaller than mice, have shovel-like front paws powered by strong legs that make the underground world habitable. They never showed up inside the cabin, but I found a pile of soil pushed up out of the ground close by—the work of a short-tailed shrew or a mole.

It turned out that the mystery beast that had pushed up the soil could be a star-nosed mole, a rare animal seldom seen except in pictures. I was anxious to see the real thing. There was only one way, and so I set a snap trap in a depression at the hole, baited it with a piece of meat, and then placed an upside-down metal dishpan over it all, to make sure I'd not accidentally catch anything from above. An hour or two later I checked, and to my great surprise I had caught a short-tailed shrew (*Blarina brevicauda*).

This common shrew species has, like other commonly underground species, no externally visible ears and only minute, pinpoint eyes. It is known for its poisonous bite. As a student I had often trapped (for cash from Turtox, a biological supply house) these shrews in tunnels under the fallen leaves in summer and fall and under the snow in winter. Might *this* individual be using a mole's tunnel to find food and shelter, parasitizing the mole's underground domain and getting away with it by its threat of a painful bite? Why is the short-tailed shrew the only mammal with a poisonous bite? No other shrew needs poison to feed on the usual shrew fare of insects and worms. So why does this one need poison unless as a threat to the larger, more powerful star-nosed mole in its underground warren, allowing it to be tolerated? There was no way for me to know, but I raised the possibility, leaving room for what might be—and therefore is reason to keep it in mind.

There were never any tracks of it *coming out*, though. Is this animal really down under all the time? Could remaking the upwelling with no more than a little roof be for getting air? I have left it at that, as a nugget of mystery and a reminder that I, too, was spending perhaps too much time alone in my cabin, being warmed at night with a warm rock heated on the stove, rather than out in the woods in the snow. I'd not be comfortable locked in with many of my kind, either, unlike the social ants and some bees and wasps in these woods that have evolved sociality to perfection.

Sociality requires animals to lose their identities and along with it all rights and possibilities except for tasks and (rarely) reproduction. Only one pair, the queen and her partner, reproduce, and if another should appear, she would be killed by the first. All others, the mostly "workers," are allocated to special castes as slaves or soldiers, existing only for promoting the common good. This type of communal life has evolved in a few wasps and cockroaches to become the form we call ant, bee, and termite societies. No mammal has come close to that level of evolution, although the naked mole rat, living underground in the dry hot desert areas in Africa, shows strong signs. Nevertheless, I continue to watch the doings of this apparent group of wannabe shrews and shrug in recognition of its nature.

THE LAST ICE age was geologically speaking yesterday, approximately nineteen thousand to thirteen thousand years ago, with an abrupt warming three thousand years later. We chased the retreating glaciers from about fifteen thousand to twelve thousand years into a sudden opening to the north, the home of the vast northern megafauna of woolly mammoths, woolly rhinos, cave bears, antelope, giant deer, and saber-toothed cats, so now they are gone.

Moving on was always the first option for an increasing population and decreasing resources. We moved on from where we had multiplied and settled where we could find space, farther into the desert, into the forests, across the seas, or onto an island, one after another where there was food, space, living room, and, for a while, *peace*. There we adapted, took on new ways, and prospered until then again reducing the plenty by becoming the too many.

One of the major selective pressures all animals of the north face, aside from the cold and getting enough solar radiation, is keeping the caloric balance in the positive. It is solved by *storing food*. I suspect that the people commonly called Neanderthals would have most closely followed what they superficially most closely resembled: bears. Bears would already have used spaces for overwintering much as we do. Furthermore, a safe overwintering place would have been someplace to sleep long and soundly. It might have been done with a good coat of fur and a good layer of fat, and fire.

Fat is hugely important. No bear could overwinter without a good layer of it, and indeed the females have even fat enough to produce milk all winter and nurse a couple of cubs. Could Neanderthals have done the same? If not, why not? It seems to me it would be *highly* unlikely they'd pass up such an obvious option, and any Neanderthal would likely be most interested in another of the opposite sex that can at least be a provider or become a parent, come spring. If so, then a sign of beauty would have been what we now derisively see as obesity.

After the first adaptation to spend winter in semihibernation was well in place, another wave of migration north could have brought new people from the south, hunters of big game, who, not being furry themselves, might have regarded those that were as bearlike. (Skinned bears, I have been told, look even more humanlike.) I suspect that the young ones might have been taken as pets, while adults were fair game. Adult Neanderthals would have been hunted as bears, especially if they lived in dwellings like bears—but were easier to remove than bears.

Killing mammoths and mastodons without rifles would not have been easy work, nor was it less cruel. More than anything else, it would have required social cooperation to survive. That meant community, social identity, residency, and territoriality. It likely led, after the megafauna was killed off and the climate warmed, to settlements.

THE MAIN PROBLEM of living in a northern winter (for those of us incapable of suspending life for a while) is finding calories. Storing a surplus in the fall to last through winter is an option; however, most organisms are already constrained getting enough in a time of plenty. Putting food away for the future without it being taken and used by another is always a gamble, one usually not worth taking.

Yet, some specialize in it, such as ground squirrels in underground larders, or honeybees in the fortresses of hollow trees while living there among a horde of defenders armed with poison or pain-inducing chemicals. Plants do the near equivalent, storing resources underground in their roots that are specially enlarged for that purpose, such as the "bulbs" or the "tubers" of potatoes. The roots of trees such as maples send up sugars for leaf, flower, and bud growth at the first warming days of spring. Many mammals have hit on the same strategy of bodily energy storage, of which the best known locally are the fall fattening of raccoons, skunks, and bears. These mammals confront this problem head- (if not belly-) on, but there is not a primate of tropical origin adapted for it. Perhaps our living in caves was an early strategy copied from bears, but soon there may not have been enough caves available to satisfy the demand. Inhabiting old trees is the functional equivalent used by a variety of mammals, including fishers, raccoons, squirrels, porcupines, and many birds, such as woodpeckers, nuthatches, and chickadees. Some woodpeckers make homes specifically for overwintering, but then make better ones in spring for raising their young. The natural hollows arising from old age in very large trees used to be where chimney swifts nested in colonies, but such trees are rare now, and so are the swifts.

There is only one ancient yellow birch tree in the woods near my cabin that is big enough for a human to crawl into, and like bears who went from caves to making crude shelters, so did I. My log cabin built in 1980 is almost entirely from spruce logs, using them to enclose a space, which bears do, too. A factor for us for living in the woods and making better shelters is an axe and several saws, and the key—an energy source—is wood. Yet recently, I read news of another breakthrough for the fusion energy that fuels the sun, as hydrogen atoms in its core fuse to produce helium. If successful, it would be scary, because it would provide nearly unlimited resources for this one species alone, to spread ad infinitum into the Northern Forest, and progress for "onward" would be going backward.

It is now a world of *our* making, showing signs that remind us of a plague of locusts, which proceed to consume all they can until they no longer have a home and must invade another's. That scenario has existed ever since we became the "sapiens," searching for another green pasture, for energy moving from coal, to gas, to oil, to nuclear fission, and now to direct capture of solar energy, to nuclear fusion.

Part V

Returning

Thirteen

A Residence for Carnivores

All kinds of creatures form tight-knit societies in winter, even those that don't crash a cozy cabin and even those that don't need to seek warmth.

WINTER WORLD, 2003

IT IS NOT ACCIDENTAL THAT THERE IS A PHOTO OF the moose (*Alces alces*) on the wall of my log cabin. It is shown sauntering by a window, a treat, as it is not routine to see a moose in these woods. In the winter of that photo, my Winter Ecology students came as usual for their ten-day North Woods immersion, and one of them wanted to see a moose, or at least she asked for one. I instructed her that the best way might be to go out and look for one. She agreed, but after an hour or so, when she was on her way back, one strolled right by the cabin, and we got it on camera. She, of course, had failed to see any, because she had unknowingly driven it up the hill.

I remember seeing a few. Once, two walked under my tree stand in deer hunting season. Another time a bull stared me down, and I made tracks to and onto the nearest tree. That's it for the live ones in the woods. Most of the ones I'd seen were walking along the road. One of those had started trotting, and I followed it a mile or so before it gave up trying to outrun me and stepped off into the woods. It had found the open road offering the least resistance and easiest traveling, but apparently not realizing that the same applied to me in my pickup truck. Moose are not known for smarts. I have seen more dead than live moose. Trucks don't slow down very fast, and moose are hard to miss.

Moose are easy to track in the winter, where their huge poundage leaves ample evidence of their passing, along with their lower sharp-ended, square teeth scraping off the bark of a species of maple tree, appropriately named *Acer pennsylvanicum*, or "moose maple." In recent winters I have tracked moose simply by following the line of red blood dots on the snow, exuding from the wounds of one affected by the winter ticks.

I've seen more moose killed by ticks than by trucks. This now famous moose tick, once it gets onto a moose, multiplies like any animal would in a safe habitat with no predators and in the presence of unlimited food. The exact number of ticks to kill a moose has not yet been determined, but it is astronomical and has been counted to within a thousand or two, or three.

One such moose fell dead in the woods about two hundred yards from where my deer hunting partner, Charlie, and I have a favorite deer stand on top of a huge rock overhang. Another died close to the cabin, but I didn't know about it at all until the water from my well tasted foul, and I then found the remains in a fir thicket fifty yards upslope from my well.

I have seen worse. Many years later, my water was again unpalatable. I found a cow moose directly *in* the well, where she had probably drowned less than an hour or two before. She had entered the well headfirst, and all I could see was her hind end sticking up a foot or so above the water. I didn't drink that water for a month or so, but got help from Mike Pratt, a friend in town who then owned the garage and had a machine with a lift. I entered the well and attached the chain to her hind legs still sticking up out of the water, and Mike winched her up and out.

The bodies of the moose all vanish quickly regardless of their imposing size (up to around fifteen hundred pounds). Those killed in winter and spring are found by carnivores—coyote, bobcat, fisher—and then the ravens, bald eagles, crows, and turkey vultures. After the snow melts, if there is anything left, the moose skeletons are cleaned by millions of maggots; then the remaining hard parts are taken by beetle larvae, and birds take the fur to line their nests. I'm not sure what takes the bones, but they disappear quickly. I suspect coyotes take some meat, given that their feces often resemble densely packed hair sausages.

For me, however, a freshly dead moose had given me the gift of a lifetime. This dead moose had been about two-thirds of a mile up the hill from my cabin, up on a mountain ridge, where it attracted the ravens, and the ravens me. It was covered with brush by (I presume) a poacher who'd taken most of it. Until then I'd not seen ravens routinely, and when I did, maybe one or two. Had one found it and announced it to the rest? If so, that seemed preposterous from current theory; these were not like bees, ants, or termites, part of a social hive.

Ravens were rare and usually solitary. The carcass I found was fresh and well hidden. Not all these birds could have found it. I would have expected if one had, it would have kept it a secret or at the very least chased competitors away as soon as one arrived. Something else had happened here. Ravens are smart. Had they figured out something humans didn't know about, maybe about sharing? But I only knew of one raven pair nesting locally within miles. There was a discovery to be made. Might the ravens have a recruitment behavior? If so, what, and why?

I'd end up spending hundreds of hours in snow-covered dens of spruce and fir branches, setting out calf and even cow carcasses, to see what might happen when a raven found the food bonanza. It was hard, and it is hard for me to imagine now how anyone, and that includes me, could have spent days in what amounted to a hole in the ground covered with a layer of balsam fir or spruce branches under snow, peeking out to see if a raven would stay silent or "yell" to advertise its find. Would a raven crowd assemble?

I could not pass up the opportunity of perhaps learning something new of their social behavior. It sparked a kinship with them leading to camaraderie with human friends and enthused us with mega prospects with these mega birds. For me it became total immersion into the Northern Forest, confronting one of the most intelligent of birds and a species with an association with humans as long as ours have been with wolves that became dogs. It led to knowing a wild animal species we could begin to understand, despite its quite different exterior. It yielded discoveries, published in science journals in collaboration with colleagues and good friends and two books of our adventures in the North Woods, where the raven is the master of its domain, with its playpen the sky. Meanwhile, other North Woods inhabitants leave tracks in the snow and retreat underground into a secret world below the frost, a place of safety from the hungry carnivores above and a refuge from the howling snow that acts like a blanket to hibernators that sleep there most of the winter. The ravens' way led to cooperation among the birds to exploit the dying and the dead as their sustenance, their food.

RAVENS HAD "TAKEN" me from my professorship at UC Berkeley to my return to Maine. I'd followed the ravens. It was a new world, but also the one I'd left behind. I was home again, having explored the worlds of different animals and becoming ever more interested and involved in the animal that is me and my kind. I'd spent a full year and a month in the mountain forests of Tanzania and three more elsewhere in the wildernesses of Africa; I'd studied in Papua, New Guinea, Ellesmere Island (in the High Arctic), Russia, Germany, Australia, and several weeks in Alaska. Throughout it all, our species seemed ever more of interest.

Our way to world success came from taming fire, an invention that came north with us out of Africa and allowed us to live in the Northern Forest. We could rally around it as a protection from carnivores, use it as a shield and a weapon to repel them from *their* kills, use it for warmth and to make our own food more nutritious, delicious, and easier to digest. We used it not just for cooking but also to avoid being eaten ourselves, as I was reminded by an adventure sixty years ago, one night around a campfire by a watering hole on Mount Meru, a long extinct crater in Kenya. We heard big animals nearby in the dense forest as they traveled the much-used paths of cape buffalo, rhino, and elephant, but we felt safe roasting an antelope over a fire that we almost clung to and where we were able to sleep.

It may be a stretch, but given some extrapolation, I think it possible that we, originating from the plains and relatively open acacia woodlands of Africa sprinkled with baobab trees, did not venture into and live in the Northern Forest year-round strictly because we liked a lot of trees around us. Living year-round in the Northern Forest would have been a severe challenge.

So why didn't we stay in Africa, our home?

It wasn't for the scenery. In Africa, at least to me, nothing appealed more aesthetically than the open acacia plains I experienced in four countries there, loaded with all of its varied life—as megafauna, birds, and reptiles. Africa also appealed to others, so much so that its bounties inevitably became contested by neighboring tribes. Some humans fled into the deep dank forests, others into the hot deserts, and still others up into the mountains. Waves of us at times went north, and then ever farther north, escaping from danger by the push of the "others" who were the enemy.

I suspect that wherever we could multiply became a desirable place, but we eventually had to leave because we were "successful," depleting the game as we became too numerous. Why else live in a dense forest of cold winters, the dry searing heat of deserts, the dense jungles, or, for that matter, the High Arctic, spending months in darkness at subzero temperatures?

IN TERMS OF emotions, survival instincts, and social bonds, the people who lived then, given the example of the 3.2-million-year-old Lucy fossil, were not likely much different from who we are now, and they would have noticed and wondered, thought, and likely come to the "obvious" conclusion, given the facts at hand. We would then, when relatively locally confined for our resources, have been highly conscious every fall of the approach of winter. Fall would have been the reminder that "it—the cold and the hunger—is coming soon!" And on the shortest day of the year, we would celebrate, because every day from then on would finally be longer, a sign by the heavens to celebrate a resurrection, the return of the sun, an imagined power that we could not have had the slightest clue of what *it* might be, except of it being unearthly and life-giving, and so we may, I suspect, have worshipped it through the ages. We saw and felt the sun that brought us everything, as summer does after winter. It never failed in its schedule, made all things grow and warmed us.

HERE AT MY cabin, looking through a window, I know precisely *where* on what spot on a hill in the horizon the sun rises on December 21, the winter solstice, the day of the first small step when we finally begin to come out of the gloom and the days finally start to get longer. That is the day of the year I celebrate above all others, and that is the day the ancient Druids may have celebrated also, until it was co-opted by the Christian religion and hence called "Christmas."

I follow the sun daily, as it rises earlier in the morning in midwinter at the base of Kinney's Head, a hill to the east, and then every day comes up a tiny bit farther to the north, then each day reaches higher into the sky, making a greater arch. It is a clock of the seasons, a reminder of the renewal of life. I don't doubt that it also served as that reminder to celebrate the renewal of life five thousand years ago, when people of the forest were directly dependent upon it. There would have been no bananas from Costa Rica, no rice from China, and no fruit from California available merely on a wish, dream, or demand.

WE, IN OUR massive populations, can now affect the climate, not just the earth under our feet. We are safe at the moment, so long as we have airplanes, trucks, and fuel to bring us food—fall, winter, spring, *and* summer—from the ever-farther ends of the earth, acting as if there is no winter. Beginning with the summer solstice, we start to lose the sun as Earth changes its course, heading us toward the freezing cold and the darkness, preceded by signals that all animals heed, as they must to succeed.

Birds prepare by fattening up to be able to fly thousands of miles, some from the far north to the far south, in a few days. Most insects, except for some rare exceptions, such as the monarch butterfly, start making their antifreeze to survive. Plants store food in underground roots and tubers, ready to make new leaves and shoots as soon as the ground thaws in the spring. Having evolved in the tropics, for us such *senses* are not needed. We can prepare from knowing.

Robert Frost famously wrote that his wood, planned for the winter, warmed him "thrice." I'm warmed even more times by mine. It is right before blackfly season in spring when I can get "het up" just by swatting them while walking around in the woods carrying a chain saw fueled with gasoline, looking for trees to fell, delimb, cut to carriable sections, then lift onto the back of the pickup, drive back to the woodpile, unload, cut into foot-long sections, split, and stack them all to dry, which is almost all there is to it, even before the thrice-warmed part in the fall.

We are made differently than our close cousin the bear, who *needs* to become obese by fall to survive winter, slowly thinning back down, and in spring starting all over again, preparing for the next winter. The wood frog (*Rana sylvatica*), who crawls under some leaves and freezes solid, is not a recommended winter survival model for us, nor for the bear, although I have heard rumors of people who've tried to mimic the strategy (though not when in the pink of health). I suspect there are no positive results of human whole-body freezing so far, but in any case, stepping into a jet plane is perhaps more appealing, although it does not begin to compare with the adventures we can enjoy vicariously from other animals following nature's mind-bending feats, and that include nonstop flights fleeing winter to a beginning spring elsewhere, and vice versa. Extremes seem to be a pattern, where the goal can only be reached by going all the way in one direction, but if not, then maybe all the way in another direction.

One of my favorite examples is an insect whose males fly in the woods only in late fall. I see them when walking around in the Northern Forest after the leaves are down and just before snow may start to fall. They appear to be tiny, tan-colored butterflies. However, there are no butterflies flying then, and these are the males of a moth, *Operophtera bruceata*, of the family Geometridae, named for the caterpillars that walk as if they are measuring their lengths rather than creeping. The adults in the fall are guaranteed to be male, searching for one thing only, females, as they do not take food. The females lack wings and mimic lumps of bark, with a butterball rotundness from their abdomen expansion by their loads of eggs, and at a glance they might be mistaken for slugs. This extraordinary sexual dimorphism seems designed for giving these moths a large advantage for being active in this season in the Northern Forest, because they emerge only after most of the insect-feeding birds have flown south. While they then face the cold, they have evolved to be active despite it; their structure permits their lifestyle.

Fourteen

Warmed Many Times Over

So perhaps I am a victim of seasonal affective disorder, with its slow-ness and melancholy. By some it is considered a pathological condi-tion, but I wonder. I'm now inclined to think it's not a disease. I think it may be a vestigial remnant of an adaptive hibernation response.

A NATURALIST AT LARGE, *2018*

FOOD IS A HUGE PROBLEM FOR MANY ANIMALS, AND it was especially so in the winter of 2023, because unlike most other years, neither the beeches nor the oaks bloomed. The American chestnut trees, in contrast, bloomed like never before—their whole tops were white. But for the first time in many years, these flowers normally pollinated by insects produced no fruit. Thus, there would be no nuts from three main sources usually relied on by the mice, squirrels, blue jays, and owls that feed on them. Even the winterberry (*Ilex verticillata*) crop was barren, although in most years these bushes are red with fruit. Birds see them even from a long distance, and last winter robins relied on them, staying almost all season. Ash, a wind-pollinated tree, had not bloomed for years, but as I observed this winter, most of the American white ash female trees (in the ash, male and female flowers are in separate trees) were resplendent in seed, and they hosted flocks of evening grosbeaks, more than I had ever seen before. But then they did not flower in the summer of 2023, so there were no seeds come winter. The red squirrels would be lacking nuts and other large seeds, but they usually have a fairly reliable seed source from cones in the tops of red spruce and white pines. Chickadees and red-breasted nuthatches then scavenge from the seed spill on the snow.

What a difference a year makes. As I write now, in October a year later, my chestnut trees have produced their largest nut crop so far. The same two trees have shed an unprecedented total of 3,778 burrs, the fruits that each normally contain three seeds (nuts). I climbed to the top of the red spruce (used in my raven studies) in the midst of as many trees, and none had even a single cone.

Changes are constant, but I had no idea how constant until taking notes, even though I'm aware by the old homestead cellar holes that forest without end became open fields, pastures, and gardens. Where I live now there was within moments of human history a forest without end—it was taken down by axes, crosscut saws, and fire, then trodden by sheep and cattle, and so came to be free and open. Masses fleeing a by then already overcrowded Europe rushed in.

In the New England of just "yesterday," scattered villages of Indigenous peoples lived by hunting and fishing and perhaps growing some squash, beans, and corn. Their lifestyle was sustained by the floodplains along rivers, such as the Kennebec, Androscoggin, and Penobscot. People came from Europe because they could, and stayed because they had better weapons. Steel saws, axes, and fire opened up and then eliminated the forestland that had been unavailable before. The forest, the "wilderness," was the enemy to the Europeans unfamiliar with it, something to be conquered. Given the new tools, this land was perceived as "free for the taking," and in the flash of an eye in geological terms, we multiplied to the millions.

Here where I live, I see both what it was like and what it became in a near "instant" of time, and how and why it changed and changes still. What happened here is what happened across much of the continent. There always seemed to be more land, more work for a living just a bit farther on.

In the mid-eighteenth century, the Swedish Academy of Sciences commissioned Peter (Pehr) Kalm to travel widely throughout North America, where he recorded seemingly everything he encountered in his *Travels in North America* (1771). I was especially intrigued by how he notes that in America "people multiply more here than in Europe. As soon as a person is old enough, he may marry in these provinces, without any fear of poverty; for there is such a tract of good ground yet uncultivated, that a new-married man can, without difficulty, get a spot of ground, where he may sufficiently subsist with his wife and children." And: "The taxes are very low, and . . . the liberties he enjoys are so great, that he considers himself as a prince in his possessions!" He further writes about a woman who died in 1742, aged ninety-seven, who left "five children, sixty-one grandchildren, one hundred and eighty-two great grandchildren, and twelve great-great-great grandchildren, who were all alive when she died."

Kalm's observations (while he stayed for a while in Raccoon, New Jersey) put me in mind of the historical novel *Come Spring*, published in 2000, and written by Ben Ames Williams, of the Adams family, to which I have a strong connection. Floyd and Leona Adams and their three boys Jimmy, Billy, and Vernon were our first close friends in Maine. There is an Adams cemetery five miles from my cabin, and the property I live on was indicated on earlier maps as Adams' Hill. Almost all the land around was recently (within a century, until people moved out West) fields and pastures. My hometown, Wilton, a running distance from where I live now, is almost a ghost town from what it used to be; the industries that had supported it have gone, every one of them, overseas. The sign coming into Wilton read "Welcome to Wilton, a Good Place to Live, Work and Play." It once was. But soon after the farms left, even the lumber mills left for bigger mills with cheaper labor in other countries. Nevertheless, nostalgia stays and may even grow, then be preserved—in poetry.

My favorite poet, Robert Frost, had something to say about this in "The Wood-Pile," where while sauntering in a swamp on a snowy day he finds a cord of maple, "cut and split / And piled— and measured, four by four by eight." (He is writing of the people of the Northern Forest, showing that he knows what a "cord" is and that he is a native, too.) The wood pile was held up on one side by a tree, and someone had left the wood because it was infected "With the slow smokeless burning of decay." Quite obviously, the wood pile represents not only wood but a pile of hard work that a woodcutter had left behind, and no one needs to be told why such work is done for a future in mind, as living in the North Woods is impossible without.

I love his poem and think of it often when I'm getting my wood. The slow disintegration of decay is to be avoided as work wasted, and I want its heat to be released not in decay but in fire in my stove. I'll savor the flame, though I was previously warmed by the cutting of the trees, the hauling, the piling, the sawing of it into foot-long lengths, the packing of it into the woodshed so it will dry and be available for the fire to release its solar energy, collected from the sun by its green leaves over many years, all from the nuclear reactions in the core of the sun, thanks to that special chemical in plants: chlorophyll. Can there be life on Earth without it?

At odd moments when I'm sitting by the flames, I think of the panorama of this forest, land, trees, and sun. I'd dragged logs on the path through these woods, which had two centuries ago been a road used by a horse carriage to get to the neighboring town from this (then) farm. A century ago, much of this countryside was overgrown by pastures with cattle, but it is all forest now, with pines near a hundred feet tall and five feet thick. Under them are now maple and birch straining to catch up, but they never will, not to a pine tree. Every year more of the neighboring trees and understory get shaded, more die, and I take them first. Those remaining trees I rescue from their death-dealing neighbors so that next spring they can finally have an opportunity to spread wide and high. They will continue their lives full force as members of this forest. I look ahead to the ever-mighty white pines, sugar maples, and now also American chestnut trees, each growing a yard or more in several directions in each short summer. I remember seeing the hundreds of little ones crowded within a square yard of ground. They are all there, all battling upward, and each and every year over 99 percent of them die for not being able to reach the sunshine. If I take out enough, and leave enough, then in a century or two this forest, once pasture, now forest again, will still have giants. I'm warmed not just once by those trees I take, but many times over by seeing the future of those remaining.

EARLY SPRING IN the Northern Forest is the birthing time of many animals. It must be, to give them time to be independent by autumn, then to be able to survive the harshness and strain of the coming winter. Usually, the earlier the start the better, and by April most mammals are starting their lives ex utero and growing, thanks to their mother's milk. Birds arrive even faster. They can't afford to be tardy, because their young need to be able to fly thousands of miles by fall to reach the warm climes of the tropics. Insects, depending on the kind, have specific developmental stages adapted to survive winter. It may be the egg, larva, pupa, or adult, depending on the species. Amphibians are constrained by longer development time, and they may spend a substantial portion of their lives in cold torpor. One of the most proficient at it and most vocal and conspicuous are the wood frogs.

All local frogs escape winter (so to speak) by taking a long nap—burrowing into the mud in a pond and staying cool and not breathing (much). They get enough oxygen through their skin and don't need much to remain comatose, waking up and hopping along as they always do come spring. Those that freeze solid can go without oxygen.

We humans are somewhat fishlike early in our development in the womb, where we get nourishment and oxygen from the mother's bloodstream, at least until we are born—and then we're supported for a good long time beyond. Wood frogs do it differently. They lay their eggs in a pool of cold water, and their young hatch from the eggs as embryo-like fish that are on their own. The pool may, however, dry up, which is an advantage: It almost guarantees that the babies aren't eaten by fish. The problem is that many, if not most, of the pools in the Northern Forest dry up too quickly, before the fishlike tadpoles have developed legs to hop out.

I happen to have a pool adjacent to my cabin, and it is fun to watch the "frog show" that starts with the loud calling of the males almost immediately after the snow and ice melt, and they summon females to engage in wild, exuberant sex.

The females have their eggs ready by fall, and they carry them all winter, so as soon as there is water in the spring, they are ready to deposit their eggs. In 2023, as expected, they provided me with entertainment, starting from the moment of their awakening on my birthday, April 19. Until then I'd led an active life splitting wood and keeping my cabin warm, but meanwhile eating up more food than during the summer and fall combined. The frogs couldn't have had a bite of food for half the year, but each female had over a thousand eggs ready since the previous October (as I discovered after finding one once under some leaves).

On their awakening day in April, while the snow was still melting, they headed for the pool, where the males began their well-known quacking concert. My pool is about a 250-square-foot hole in the ground that was this year filled to the brim with snowmelt, although there was at that time, at the beginning of their concert, still a two-foot-thick layer of snow on the shaded side in the woods.

No eggs had yet been deposited when I watched them on their first chorus of the year, and I predicted, correctly, the location where all the eggs would later end up in a huge pile. That communal egg pile was then, as always, attached to the topmost twigs of vegetation in the water, at the *least* shaded site, the one with most access to sunshine. The next day I found dozens of egg masses exactly where I had expected.

Then the spectacle occurred. The males were as usual at that time spread out over the top of the pool and calling in mutual on and off bellows of several minutes to an hour. There were soon nineteen egg masses in a clump along shore. But totally unexpected was a noisy whirl of frogs locked together into a ball at the bottom of the pool just below an egg mass. As I retrieved it and held it in my hand, the male frogs refused to separate from the clump. They stayed locked together while continually making croaking noises, their forelegs clamped solidly around the female who was then extruding her egg clutch after perhaps having fallen off the nearby communal egg dump. The communal egg mass may be crucial for fertilization, and in confirmation I retrieved a single loose egg clump (one from one frog only) in the water below the main egg mass, to test its viability; its eggs did not hatch, whereas others taken at the same time (also fresh) from the main pile did hatch. I suspect it had not been fertilized.

Additionally with all the eggs deposited into one communal egg pile, rather than separately, males coming there to fertilize them are potentially fertilizing the eggs of more than one female at once in their single mating of the season, and likely their lifetimes. But there is more to egg hatching than fertilization. It is temperature. Eggs retained in a large communal clump reduce water flow and increase local warming by reducing convection. And the adventure of discovery continued.

Fifteen

Feeling the Beauty and Wonder of Nature Is a Prelude to Loving It

We are within reach of seeing and feeling the whole earth biosphere. The world, not merely our neighborhood, is now our common reality. Nature is the ultimate standard of reality, and from what has been revealed so far, I see the whole world as an Organism with no truly separate parts. I want to be connected to the grandest, biggest, most real, and most beautiful thing in the universe as we know it: the life of earth's nature.

LIFE EVERLASTING, *2012*

WANDERING IN THE NORTHERN FOREST IN ALL four seasons is a journey of unending marvels. Lofty views into the far distance inspire a sense of grandeur, but focusing on an ever-smaller scale reveals often unimaginable mechanisms of interdependence, starting at the cellular level, leading to individuals, species, and ecosystems, knitting all of life on this planet into a superorganism. Species melding has long been known with respect to lichens, each being a unique amalgam of a fungus and an alga acting and being one. Recently, a yeast has been determined to be a part of it as well. Lichens support northern reindeer, who in turn feed carnivores in a well-known pattern endlessly repeated in all ecosystems on Earth.

With life depending and feeding on other forms of life, the distinctions between exploitation, parasitization, and predation are often thin, and evolve by shifts of one to the other. Flowers evolved bright colors and scents and sweetness with sugars to attract the insects. The insects steal the flowers' pollen, and the flowers produce more seeds, necessary for their reproduction, as seeds that are taken by other predators are spread to become new plants. Plants evolved to pack seeds into fruits that are sought by animals and then dispersed. Animals that are sought by predators when they reach a population density leading to starvation are selectively reduced by predators to levels where they can once again feed and reproduce, as predators concentrate on the most common prey, especially those starving. Different components in multiple intertwining relationships have of course long been known, and for the most part understood, yet they are still yielding surprises; I did not expect such a surprise from one of our common beetles, one that buries mouse carcasses and that in flight can morph from a black beetle to its appearance as a yellow bumblebee.

The extent and evolutionary implications of the symbiosis of interspecies relationships have been revealed in ever-finer detail. They now include the structure and function of individual cells themselves. However, the symbiosis of separate and diverse organisms uniting into one body took a while to prove and to sink in and could not have been revealed without the spectacular breakthrough of the structure and mechanisms of DNA, leading to what we now see as the tree of life.

Multicelled organisms branched off to create ever-greater and diverse associations into ever-more adaptations to *specific* ecosystems. The cells of plants contain their chromosomal DNA, plus that of chloroplasts that capture the energy from the sun. Similarly, their mitochondria and ours were ancient bacteria-like parasites that survived and then thrived within their hosts, evolving to become symbiotic in an arrangement that provided energy-powering movement and then locomotion. Yet competition is a strong driving force that has shaped, and still shapes, life, and the operation of two forces makes it an interesting, often shifting balance.

Animals beyond our own species could, however, easily be *seen* to be different and therefore automatically suitable to be routinely killed and eaten. Elk, bison, giant sloths, elephants, rhinos, seals, porpoises, whales, monkeys, and innumerable others were hunted, in many cases to near extinction and in cruel ways, with little concern of how much or whether they, like us, felt pain or had emotions. Even until recently, there was pointed derision of such notions of empathy being "unscientific" and therefore invoking distancing by tangled belief constructs such as "anthropomorphisms." The "other" label, once applied, sticks by being passed on in culture like a badge worn permanently on the chest, to unite "us" by separation from "them." It is a human adaptation coded in our DNA and has no say as to what is right or wrong, only what *is* and may therefore be worth knowing. I loved Goliath, my raven friend. I loved my tame raccoon, and as a child *every* animal, even those that I hunted and set onto pins (after they were dead) for my collections. I thought of them as "different" from me yet also similar. The more I knew of them, the more I liked and then loved and wanted to be with them.

Belonging to something larger than ourselves extends us, from family to a team having a common purpose—a club, a school, a profession, an interest, a fashion, or a country. The clearer the markers of the group and knowledge of it, the larger the extent of attainment of identity, such as by wearing a uniform signifying visual proof of membership. Almost anything can serve as a marker for group identity and would then become an excuse to join, or to divide, and then shift behavior in a certain direction.

Ultimately, togetherness is the feeling of belonging to something greater than us—as a group being able to exert a force greater than that which can be produced by the individual alone. It is invoked to be constructive but can also be destructive, accelerated by our ever-increasing development of technology.

Charles Darwin, famously credited with perhaps the most important human insight into life, that of evolution, in his 1859 book, *On the Origin of Species*, wrote: "There is grandeur in this view of life—from the simple beginning endless forms of the most beautiful and most wonderful have been and are being evolved." He also wrote in an 1860 letter to botanist Asa Gray: There seems to me too much misery in the world. I cannot persuade myself that a beneficent and omnipotent God would have designedly created the Ichneumonidae with the express intention of their feeding within the living bodies of caterpillars." (Ichneumonidae is a family of wasps that reproduce by inserting an egg into another insect larva, which then consumes the host larva from the inside.) Thus, he was not portraying nature as something warm and fuzzy to embrace wholeheartedly, but only that evolution of the selfish insentient mechanical genes could have produced such a cruel process.

Implying that it could not have been a merciful God that created the ichneumon wasps may be true enough. But we may dispute the horror of their parasitism as a punishment of nature. Caterpillars are unlikely sentient to being eaten, and we might consider the ichneumon parasitism like a fairytale marvel, like the frog morphing into a prince. Ichneumon wasps are beautiful, and we might agree that many an ichneumon wasp is just as or more beautiful than many a moth. Furthermore, in some species of the ichneumon wasps, one egg deposited into a caterpillar divides itself into two, and the two eggs into four, then into eight, and then sixteen beautiful wasps are produced instead of just one moth. Beauty and magic galore.

Recent discoveries at the Mootha Laboratory, in Cambridge, Massachusetts, have revealed that life as we know it evolved literally from *one alga-like cell* some 2.5 billion years ago that became infected, parasitized, or partnered (depending on your definition) with a bacteria-like cell, one that could utilize oxygen to generate energy. That unusual combination proved to be highly superior to all others, and that bacteria-like cell in the partnership evolved to become the mitochondria that allow cells not only to tolerate the otherwise potentially poisonous oxygen, but to use it by allowing and promoting the oxidation of food. This extraordinary event happened only once—a microscopic event that changed the world forever. As Vamsi Mootha is quoted as saying in "The Cell's Power Plant," published by *Harvard Magazine* in November-December 2018, "The evolutionary success it conferred was so great that the single cell multiplied and became the ancestor of *all* plants, animals, and fungi." We are all related, all derived from the same cell that mastered the trick of a genetic code to replicate itself to produce the beautiful and fantastic through the process of natural selection that has now been proven in our century, after several billion years. Fantastic, yes. Unimaginable, no longer.

Deciphering that story has been an awesome achievement of science, and it seems to me it is one with religious implications. I cannot imagine anything more epochal or as grand: at first a solid theory based on the big picture in ecology, then with ever-more stunning confirmations in cellular biology, and on to genetics and molecular biology, with the boost within recent memory (1953) by James Watson and Francis Crick's model of double-stranded DNA. Their model was derived from the single-stranded RNA virus of the tobacco plant, its helical structure revealed by Rosalind Franklin's X-ray crystallography. Then, in May 1961, J. Heinrich Matthaei, a postdoc in the lab of Marshall Nirenberg at the National Institutes of Health, in Bethesda, Maryland, proved that there are *three* nucleic acids in a row on the DNA code for *one* amino acid of the protein chain. (In his experiment, the nucleic acid molecule uracil coded for the amino acid phenylalanine.) Nirenberg, Matthaei's mentor, announced this momentous finding (which then quickly led to the codes of all the other nineteen amino acids of proteins) at the International Congress of Biochemistry in Moscow that year. The code writing of life had been cracked.

That code of every living thing, all of life on Earth, is built on the same genetic platform. The DNA sequence and length are indeterminate and vary endlessly. Our own DNA has 3.2 billion base pairs, and the tiny fruit fly, *Drosophila melanogaster*, has "only" 130 million. Those base pairs code around 20,000 genes in us and 13,600 in the fly. Now we have the technology for reading the whole DNA sequences of ourselves and increasingly others, and ours differs by only 1.2 percent from a chimpanzee's. We are related to all, each of us an amalgam of perhaps whole ecosystems of different organisms cooperating together in our body, and our bodies with others in the broader ecosystem, and the ecosystems affecting each other.

The energy-generating mitochondria that power our muscles are ancient parasitic bacteria that went on to evolve to help rather than harm their hosts, as do those many species present in our digestive tract that aid in digestion, as well as those in our skin and immune system and also including ancient viruses that are now essential in the female placenta and that in males may help in muscle development. Plants became plants perhaps from something like fungi that had been invaded by single-celled algae, then chloroplasts capturing energy from sunlight and instigating the evolution of plants, and then plants and animals exploiting each other, evolving similar systems that involve whole ecosystems, living as mutually dependent parts on the soil, in waters, and in forests and together acting globally, affecting climate.

One of the greatest thrills I had as a biologist is how the ravens *proved* to me (in my experiments) that they could *think*. Thinking was, I believed, the most important trait we had that lifted us somehow *above* others; but by lessening the distance between *us* and *them*, I could perceive more worthy potential friends "out there" and thus be less alone. We don't make "the system." Nature does, and *it* is the *real*.

We can modulate locally, but ultimately, we rely on the tried and true, and the more tampering of the system, the more likely a disruption of the structure that took billions of years to evolve. All evolved to promote their genes in preference to those of others in the context of their environment, which for us includes a social contract we identify with. But how far will it reach as our world shrinks?

I'm confident that the consequences of the scientific method will eventually unite us all against not our creatively invented enemies, but our real enemies. Those ancient genes still have a strong hold on us so long as we do not acknowledge life on Earth as a unity, as did the English ecologist James Lovelock (1919–2022) in his famous Gaia hypothesis, where Earth is a superorganism, the atmosphere and oceans being the circulation, and a body of fields and forests, with flora and fauna, now suffering a fever, and us a virus, as the cause.

Embracing nature has often been seen as unpalatable, as English poet Alfred Lord Tennyson suggests with his famous words "Nature, red in tooth and claw" in his poem "In Memoriam A.H.H.," an elegy upon his dear friend's sudden death. Tennyson hedged with the thought that they would later be reunited in heaven, writing, "Thou wilt not leave us in the dust" not far from his point in "Ulysses" that "I am a part of all that I have met."

How many of us have deliberately met nature?

Many! And the number is growing as new revelations of its intricate beauty and grandeur continue to emerge, far beyond euglenas and even wood frogs, racoons, and ravens.

Feeling the beauty and wonder of nature is a prelude to loving it and achieving a state of grace by the knowledge of being a part of something beyond ourselves, being linked to every other organism. Unity, worth, and beauty are assured forever in a continuing chain of connectedness stretching into the future as long as we cherish life. It is seeing a connection that began when the first cells joined one another in sex to make variation and hence made evolution possible with then no end in sight. It is being or becoming an active part of immortality. I want to be a part of and connected to the grandest, biggest, most real, and most beautiful thing in the universe as we know it: the life of Earth's nature. I want to join the party of the greatest show on Earth, life everlasting.

ACKNOWLEDGMENTS

WRITING THIS BOOK HAS BEEN FOR ME A JOURNEY through the thickets or tangled bank of Darwin, back to the awakening of and by my mentors, first my father Gerd Heinrich, but then my tussle with *Euglena* in the laboratory at the University of Maine under the tutelage of the best-ever professor, James R. Cook. Directly although even more indirectly it led me to *everything* after my thesis in 1966 titled "The Physiology of *Euglena gracilis* During Substrate Induction and Repression of the Glyoxylate By-Pass." It lived on in many ways that could never have been imagined, to so many fantastic people and adventures, from cellular to global explorations. In particular I thank John Ciopolla, whose magical knowledge and patience allowed me entrance to interests that evolved to be essential to living deep in the woods. Lastly, I profited greatly from the expertise and enthusiasm of both Alice Peck and John Glusman in the editing and the writing of this book, and Sandy Dijkstra, the best agent ever. It would not have happened without them.

INDEX